HINDUISM

INDICA

HINDUISM

A VAST
TAPESTRY
of
AGE-OLD
TRUTHS

PROF. V. KRISHNAMURTHY

ISBN

Hardcase 979-8-89632-376-1
Paperback 979-8-89632-374-7

Contents

HINDUISM – A VAST TAPESTRY OF AGE-OLD TRUTHS

Preface

This is a book for those, young or old, Indian or not, to learn about the fundamentals of the ancient religion, called Hinduism. It takes you into the company of the good so that you may not be proud of wealth, kith and kin and youth. It attempts to tell you in the course of eighteen chapters how the ancients thought and researched into this problem and have arrived at a unique answer called the truths of Sanatana dharma. Try your luck!

Acknowledgements

It is a pleasure to note that the book has come to fruition not just by my effort but along with mine the team of Kavya Reddy's team has been doing a marvelous job of formatting my unformatted document and carrying out meticulously all the proof corrections I have made.

Also my family members, namely my two sons and two daughters and their spouses have been taking extreme care of my health and other needs, at this advanced age of mine. Without their care of me I would not have written this book and brought it to fruition. Long live them all!

Finally I thank the chief of Indica Mr. Karan Vadlamani who has kindly sponsored the publication of this book as he has done in ten or more of my previous books.

Foreword

Dr K. Aravinda Rao
(Retd. D.G. of Police, A.P. and Expositor at
www.advaita.academy.org)

It is a delight to get the distilled wisdom of the Upanishads in an encapsulated form from Prof. Krishnamurthy (lovingly known as Prof. VK) who studied Vedanta for about eighty years. We can say this because he was born and trained in an orthodox tradition in which he became acquainted with the concepts of Vedanta at an early age. In his mid-nineties now, he is actively contemplating the concepts of Vedanta and handing it over to the modern student. What can be more welcome than such a kind transmission to the young generation?

There is a structure in the eighteen chapters – from the externalities of religion to the metaphysical thought process of the sages. It starts with an overview of the Upanishadic thought which forms the basis for the religion which we now know as Hinduism. Hinduism is not mere belief and rituals, but it is a process of inner purification needed for spiritual ascent to realize the nature of Supreme Reality and become one with It. It is the formula given by the Gita too.

The process of ascent starts with the identification of what has to be reined in or avoided. These are the animal passions of lust, anger, hatred and such. It is interesting to note that Prof. VK has updated the evils from a modern perspective, identifying them as social evils, political evils, cultural evils etc., making it easy for the reader to connect to the Gita. Balancing human needs while checking their unbridled pursuit is what the sages advocated.

The 'Empire of the Mind' is discussed exclusively. The mind is a crucible in which science, religion and philosophy meet, says the author. The different layers of the mind have to be observed and analyzed in order to control or conquer the ego. The author discusses the ideas of free will and determinism (generally called fate) and shows how spiritual pursuit can modify the so-called fate and help the seeker. Actions like contemplation generate good vasanas which gradually become a stream, and the mind progresses freely in that stream.

The author clarifies certain intricate concepts of the Gita. For instance, the verse 18-66 of the Gita talks of 'renouncing all dharmas' and surrendering to God. What is sought to be renounced is the 'I' and 'mine'. Instead of identifying with the real 'I', which is not different from the Supreme Reality, even pundits identify 'I' with the social self. This false dharma has to be renounced, says the author. The discussion on the ego (in Ch. 9) is almost like a meditation, examining the state of mind of an enlightened person.

Similarly, the chapters on the Gita give the concepts in present day terms. For instance, karma yoga involves morality, fair play, justice, and duty. It is a very straightforward explanation for a modern student. Faith, conviction, and an attitude of surrender are the basis of bhakti yoga. But this is not the end of religion. These two are the means sine qua non for the next step, the jnana path.

The author does an impartial presentation of different schools, in addition to the non-dualist school. This is essential to give a complete picture of Indian thought.

The book is made more interesting by illustrating some personal experiences of the author about miracles and the power of mantras.

The topic of changes in the educational system has been a passion for the author in his earlier books too. Here too, he outlines certain suggestions which make education more human. Education should liberate us from our narrow identities, he says. In his very brief preface, Prof. VK says that a study and internalization of the book will transport the reader into the company of the good, taking away the pride of wealth, position in society and such trappings. He says, 'try your luck', implying that the reader too should have some luck to read Vedanta with an open mind and live the truths of

Sanatana dharma. It is time for us to dive into the book and try to uplift ourselves.

My pranams to Prof.VK for giving us such a compact book of universal truths to guide the young and old, Hindu and non-Hindu alike.

*****

HINDUISM – A VAST TAPESTRY OF AGE–OLD TRUTHS

CHAPTER 1

A Simplistic Overview of Hinduism

Hinduism is an ancient religion and one of the major religions of the world. To present it in a single essay is a formidable task. We shall highlight only the bare essentials and that too, without any sophistication.

The first distinguishing feature is that it has no founder who started the religion. Also there is no single event or sequence of events which may be cited as responsible for the founding, if any, of the religion. In this sense it differs from every other religion of the world.

According to the Vedas which are the supreme authority for everything in Hinduism, there is only one God. You may call Him by any name and give Him any form. The wise call Him by any one of several names. He is present everywhere and at all times. To refer to God as a 'He', is by itself an unintended compromise. It could be a 'She' also. To recognize this, the scriptures speak very often of Godhead rather than God and refer to that Absolute Godhead as 'It'.

This unique Godhead, this Divinity, is in everything that we see, hear, smell, touch or feel. It is in every inanimate object and also in every animate being. It is in our heart of hearts. But then why don't we see It, Him or Her? Why don't we feel the presence of this Godhead in us? It is because our minds are so impure. If we can get rid of all the impurities from the innermost recesses of our hearts, Hinduism asserts, we can certainly see God reflected in the crystalline purity of our heart and mind. To be able to see it and live in the constant awareness of the presence of that Divinity is the purpose of life. In that living presence of the reflection of God in our mind, we must get tuned to the frequency of the call of that Divinity and be of service to society; – this is what we are for.

Anything that we do which encourages or is concordant with the above process of realisation of God's presence in us is called puNya or spiritual merit. Anything that we do or think that takes us away from that realisation is called pApa or spiritual sin. Truth, non-violence, humility, compassion, sympathy, unselfish service to society, helping the poor, the depressed and the sick – these are certainly among the well-known puNyas of Hinduism, as in any other religion. If one accumulates a large amount of extraordinary puNya to his credit he goes to heaven after death, to enjoy, for a specified period of time, the fruits of his puNya. If one accumulates a large amount of extreme sin he goes to Hell, to suffer the punishment for all that sin, again for a specified period. But the large majority of humanity does not belong to either category and are only a mixture of ordinary puNyas and ordinary sins. This large majority of people are born again in this world. This last one is the second most distinguishing feature of Hinduism.

Everyone who is born has to die some time or other. But when the body dies the soul does not die.

> **Important note: When we use the word 'soul' in Sanatana Dharma, it is not the same as the 'soul' commonly known in English or other western writing. The 'soul' of Sanatana Dharma has properties totally different and distinguished from the 'soul' in occidental understanding.**

The soul is born again in another body. The mind also goes along with the soul, though it does not remember what it did in the previous body. The mind and soul, together individualized in this fashion, go on from body to body again and again. This is the unique principle of transmigration. When the soul travels like this from body to body, carrying along with it the mind which has in some sense, irrevocably, attached itself to it, the mind, on its own, carries a heavy luggage within itself, namely all the imprints of pure and impure impressions of memories and experiences which it has collected in each of its sojourns in a body. The mind is like the wind which carries the smell of a rose garden through which it has blown, even long after it has left the garden. Like the wind which has passed through a filthy and stinking place, the mind carries the stink that it has collected in its previous births and lives, into succeeding births. The soul knows no good or bad, but the mind which is with it carries all the good and bad imprints in it, which reflect themselves as the tendencies of the person in his present birth. A mind which has in its previous births helped the poor, has been sympathetic, compassionate and noble, carries such tendencies in its future lives. This is why we see some people from their very birth are very noble and gentle and some people, if we may say so, stink! Thus are born the tendencies and in-born nature of people. These tendencies are known technically as vAsanAs.

VAsanA means smell. So the smell of purity or of impurity which one carries from one's actions in one's previous lives is what distinguishes person from person even though each has the same pure Divinity in oneself. This cycle of transmigration of soul and mind will end only when man realises the presence of Divinity in himself and 'reaches' God. This will happen when his inner mind is devoid of all imprints of any kind whatsoever, in other words, devoid of all vAsanAs. This is the state of Salvation of Man. Thereafter he never has to be born again. Even souls which go to Heaven or Hell because of an extreme merit or demerit, have to come back to be born as human beings on earth in order to continue on their path of evolution. The ultimate destination of all souls is to merge in the Supreme Presence of God.

God is the only Reality which is ever present, in the past, in the present and in the future. Anything else is transient. The only Truth is God and He has no name or form. He is therefore an Impersonal Absolute, though we have used the pronoun He here. Anything that we see is His creation. When we think of Him as the Creator, we call Him Brahma (pronounced brahmA). Anything that is created has to be dissolved. When God takes up this function of Dissolution or Destruction we call Him Siva (pronounced 'shiva' – where the sh denotes the palatal 's' in the German word sprechen - , not 'siva' – where the 's' is as in 'sun' or the 'ss' in 'hiss' - nor as 'Shiva' – where the 'Sh' is as in the English word 'Show' -). When we think of Him as our protector and savior we call Him Vishnu (pronounced viShNu). The same unique Godhead of Hinduism has three major functions. The three Gods of these functions form a Trinity. But actually there is only one God which we speak of as three. Whether we worship Brahma, Vishnu or Siva, we are worshipping the same Absolute Godhead.

Since God is present in all beings and in all creations of His, He is present in all Nature. Every inanimate object is also a manifestation of His presence. So we can worship Him in any form whatsoever. This is the basis of idol worship in Hinduism and this is the third most distinguishing feature of Hinduism. God is worshipped through images, or idols or pictures of Him as imagined by us. Usually a newcomer to Hinduism is confused about this idol worship. An idol is like the flag for an army. The flag is not the country but it definitely stands for the country and one is prepared to die for it. So also an idol is a symbol of God. In fact, any symbol is good enough. The mind cannot worship in abstraction. So Hinduism says:

Worship God in any form you like, the form is not important.

The name is not to be debated.

It is the intensity of devotion to God that matters.

It is the attitude of worship, called *bhakti*, in Sanskrit, that is of real consequence. Any one of the three Gods of the Trinity can be worshipped in this way and each such worship will purify the mind, which is the objective of all worship. Worshipping an idol in the tradition of Hinduism does not mean we are worshipping that inanimate object as God in a pagan way, but it means that we are worshipping the omnipresent Divinity in the form of the idol before us. <u>We are worshipping God in the idol and not the idol as God.</u>

There is another distinguishing feature of Hinduism which is present in no other religion. Just as the three Gods of the Trinity, namely, Brahma, Vishnu and Shiva are only the same unique Godhead manifested in different functions and forms so also there are other manifestations of God in the mythological history of India. God's Will is supreme. So whenever He wants

He can appear in this world as a concrete person or being in flesh and blood. This he has done many times. In fact, every time there has been a decline of natural order in the Universe, every time there has been a rise of cruelty and evil, God has manifested Himself. Each such appearance is called an *avatar*. 'avatAr' means descent. The Impersonal Absolute Godhead descends, as it were, to the level of ordinary concrete universe and makes its presence felt in flesh and blood. The perfect God takes on, it seems, an imperfection in itself to appear as a living being in order to take us imperfect beings, on the onward path to perfection! So whenever such an event takes place, as when the Son of God appeared on earth, the people of that time who had the beatific experience of God's proximate presence, consider themselves very fortunate and worship Him as God. And this is how, every avatAr, in Hinduism, has come to be worshipped as God. These avatArs are the closest approximations to Divinity for us, who cannot see Him ourselves.

Once He appeared as Man-Lion (actually it was half-man, half-lion) – the Sanskrit word being 'narasimha' – In order to put an end to the extreme cruelty which a very powerful but inhuman king was perpetrating on the world. In fact the son of this King, just a five-year-old boy, was very devoted to Lord Vishnu but the King in his arrogance wanted himself to be recognised as the only God, the God, of this universe. After many futile attempts to convert this little boy to his viewpoint, the

King asked the child to show him this God Vishnu whom he was worshipping. In extreme desperation he showed a pillar and asked: Is your God in this pillar? The son, Prahlada, with supreme confidence in the omnipresence of the Lord, said YES.

And lo and behold! God obliged His devotee by appearing in the concrete form of a Man-Lion From that pillar! This Man-lion proved to be the end of the King. The fact that He appeared as a Man-Lion itself has a history behind it. In short, it was because the King, by his own supernatural prowess was under a beneficient spell that he could never be killed by any human being or by any being of the animal kingdom. This Man-Lion avatAr of God, which occurred for a very specific purpose, is one of the earliest avataArs of Vishnu in the mythology of India. It shows the efficacy of a full-fledged hundred per cent faith in the omnipresence of God. Prahlada is the model of such faith.

There are two most famous avatArs of God – without a knowledge of which even a summary presentation of Hinduism is not complete. These are Rama and Krishna, the two names with which the entire Hindu India will reverberate wherever you go.

Rama and Krishna, who are the divines embedded in the two epics Ramayana and Mahabharata, are the two divinities, among all such who ever walked on earth, and who have captured the hearts of the largest number of people for the longest period of time.

In the same type of thinking, Valmiki and Vyasa, the authors of the two epics mentioned, are the two authors who have influenced the largest number of people for the longest period of time, in all of history.

Millions of years ago, there lived a King, Ravana by name, who was destroying all the good things that the Rishis were doing to propitiate God for the good of humanity. His powers were so great that no ordinary divine power could match him. Finally Lord Vishnu by His own Will, was born as the son in a royal family. This son of God was known as Rama. The word Rama means in Sanskrit the Ultimate Reality of everything. Rama and his consort Sita by various circumstances underwent many sufferings by living fourteen years in the forest away from civilisation and away from luxury and comfort. Finally Rama had to fight all the evil men who worked for Ravana and in the end Ravana himself was destroyed with all his clan.

This manifestation of God as Rama is a central thread in the vast fabric of Hinduism, just as Resurrection is the central kingpin of Christianity. Rama and Jesus had many things in common. Both were a great colossus of humility without the least shade of arrogance. Both undertook suffering on themselves for the rest of humanity. Jesus died on the Cross so that humanity may be saved for God. Rama lived a life of truth, compassion and virtue throughout his long life and showed to the world how we must not only be prepared to sacrifice but in reality renounce every single attachment of ourselves, for the happiness of the rest of the world.

The avatAr of Krishna happened five thousand years ago in the city of Mathura in North India. Again it was the same purpose: Protection of the virtuous and punishment for the wicked. Krishna's story has several parallels with the life of Jesus. The birth itself was a miracle. And in his life Krishna performed several miracles. Once he had to carry a whole hill on his shoulders in order to protect the entire community from destruction through Nature's fury.

Krishna's life in another sense is most important for Hinduism because He condensed all the truths and philosophy of Hinduism in a few hundreds of simple verses and taught it directly to one of the most well-known characters in the history of Hinduism, namely, Arjuna. This teaching is called the Bhagavad-Gita,the Song of the Lord or the Divine Song or Poem. (Go to chapter 13 of this book) In fact for those who cannot go back to the entire Vedas to understand Hinduism, the Gita has everything in it. It is very much relevant in the modern context.

The final teaching of the Gita is:

Do your work in an unselfish way.

Even if your duty leads you on to do apparently unjustifiable things, put the burden on God and do your duty.

Do not keep on worrying about what is going to happen in the future.

Have faith in the ultimate Divinity of every being.

Love and serve every being.

Each being has the same Divinity in them as what you have in you.

If you serve God and humanity with humility and surrender to the Will of God

You have nothing to fear, either in this life or in the after-life.

Do not be carried away by the ups and downs of everyday life.

And leave the problem of Salvation to God.He will take care of it.

The really most distinguishing feature of Hinduism is, however, that it is a matter of faith with the Hindus to consider all religions as true. Since God can be worshipped in several forms and several ways, Hinduism considers different religions as so many paths to God. No religion should think that it is the only true religion. Each is a path to the same one God. And so there should be no hate or distrust of another religion or another point of view with respect to God. In this modern world of strife and hatred this tolerance of other religions and other points of view with respect to God is one of the major lessons that the world has to learn from the Hindu way of life. Even within Hinduism, you can choose that path which suits your taste, evolution, training and tradition. The only thing that is important is there should be no feeling of selfishness or egoism.

CHAPTER 2

First Steps on the Spiritual Ascent to the Divine

Recognize the Animal Passions of the human species

*AhAra-nidrA-bhaya-maithunaMca sAmAnyaMetad-
paSubhir-narANAM /*

*dharmo hi teshAM adhiko viSeshaH dharmeNa hInAH
paSubhis-samAnAH //*

from Hitopadesha in Sanskrit

'Hunger, sleep, insecurity and sex urge are common to men and animals but the understanding of dharma is the extra quality of man which makes what a man is'. Without dharma he is just an animal. The word dharma may be loosely translated as: duty or pursuit of social and personal ideals of behaviour. It is one of the untranslatable words in Hindu scriptural literature. It has many more connotations. If the only enjoyment a man knows is that of physical sensations, then he is only a dressed-up walking animal, though a thinking animal. One of the 1330 couplets of the world-famous Tamil classic, tirukkuraL, an invaluable guide to the art and science of good living, written in the first century

A.D., has this beautiful thought on the same topic: 'Food, clothing and the like are not anything special for beings, but the sense of shame (in doing wrong) is what is special to mankind'. (Kural #1012)

OonuDai echam uyirkellAm vEralla; nANudamai mAndar chirappu. (Tamil)

Animals probably will never understand man's precocity for clothing, because they have no sense of shame. What distinguishes man from animals is not only the physical sense of shame but a spiritual sense of shame The Sanskrit language has an interesting word for this: hrIh. This is the word which Adi SankarAcArya (to be referred to as Sankara very often) interprets in his commentary on sanat-sujAtIyaM, as *akArya-karaNe lajjA*, meaning shame in doing what ought not to be done.

The concept of spiritual sense of shame has, inbuilt into it, the concept of spirituality. One might hasten to think that we are bringing in the idea of spirituality rather extraneously. So first let us clear what we mean by spirituality. What is spirituality? Man has two kinds of mental attitudes, yet he is essentially divine, say the Hindu scriptures. But it is his animal instinct that is more prominent most of the time. His divine instinct shows up very rarely, if at all. The animal instincts are those that have been cultivated over several lives. To fight against these and resume permanently one's natural divine instinct, is the purpose of life. *The pursuit of the divine instinct in oneself, by oneself, for the benefit of one's own self, is spirituality.* This spirituality is to be won step by step by personal effort. It penetrates into one's heart, changes attitudes and purifies all relationships. But why spirituality? In this mundane world of rat-race for prosperity and one-up-manship there are many who think that talking about the need for spirituality is nonsense. Spirituality, according to them, does not give man bread and butter nor does it provide him the other comforts of life without which he cannot live. This kind of thinking refuses to comprehend why spirituality is needed – just as, animals do not understand man's need for clothing. Need for clothing will be understood only if the concept of shame is understood. Need for spirituality will be felt only if the concept of inner life or consciousness is understood. If we do not understand this, we are like animals.

The animal in us brings with it **six evils** which are rooted in the human mind. They are usually recognised as the animal passions in man and constitute the major obstacles in the ascent to spirituality. These are:

Lust or any desire that is illegitimate; Attachment and head-long passion for one's possessions, belongings, kith and kin and opinions; Hate; Anger; Greed; and Confusion and delusion.

These are known, in Sanskrit, as: kAma, rAga, dvesha, krodha, lobha and moha, respectively.

The human mind has perfected these individual evils over several millenia rather persistently and successfully.

In addition to these six, the human mind nurtures **six more evil tendencies** – for which man cannot blame his animal ancestry. These are

Arrogance; Jealousy, the feeling of discomfort at another's rise or success; The awkward feeling, 'why my miseries are not happening to others?'; Spite or Malice – the feeling that does not brook or give any credit to others even when they have legitimately deserved it and so takes pleasure in talking them down; Fad for show – a projection of one's own name or personality in everything that happens; and Pride, the feeling that nobody else is equal to oneself.

These six are known, in Sanskrit, by the words, mada, mAtsarya, IrSyA, asUyA, dambha and garva, respectively.

These twelve evils or diseases of the mind as we may call them, are all captained, monitored, motivated and prompted by a grand master – the EGO. It is referred to as 'aham-kAra' in Sanskrit. Nobody escapes it. It is the king-pin of all villainy. It is the source of all evil tendencies in man's mind. But it is not as if it is unconquerable. By constant practice and dispassion, say the scriptures, one can control these twelve evil tendencies along with their captain, the Ego. By thought the ego was made and so by thought the power of the ego can be unmade. But the thought must now be directed toward a higher entity, for the ego would never allow itself to be attacked. In order that one may succeed in this endeavour, one has to channel the mind toward the only two good tendencies in Man which can oppose each one of the thirteen, with some success. These two are:

- **Faith; and**
- **Devotion-cum-dedication.**

The Sanskrit words for these are: SraddhA; and, bhakti. Faith is faith in the divinity of the Self within each one of us. Devotion to that Inner Self and dedication to everything that represents that dvinity together constitute the bhakti that is natural to us. But the thirteen evil tendencies in the mind create obstacles for the expression of this devotion and dedication. Not only do they create obstacles but they pull us in exactly the opposite direction, away from the divinity that is inherent in us. It is therefore necessary to exercise our willpower (icchA) and extricate the intellect from the clutches of the Ego and its entire gang of twelve. The will-power has to be trained to recognise the ego everytime it rears its head and to say, 'Hey e-go, you go!'

In actuality it is the presence and domination, in each one of us, of this gang of twelve led by their captain, the Ego, that is responsible for the several evils, social and cultural diseases of the society. These evils can be classified under five heads as follows:

- **Ten sociological diseases**: Gambling , Robbery, Drinking, Smoking, Murder, Suicide, Rape, Divorce, Drug Addiction and Pollution of Environment.
- **Five political evils**: Corruption, Nepotism, Hypocrisy, Turncoatism and Loose values.
- **Five economic evils**: Slavery, Beggary, Luxury, Poverty and Exploitation.
- **Five cultural evils**: Dogmatism & Bigotry, Religious prejudice, Race or caste prejudice, Superstition and Male domination.

These evils are all rooted in one or more of the individual bad tendencies that we listed earlier. In fact each of the 25 evils of the society can be carefully analysed and traced to individual weaknesses in the members of the society which express themselves collectively because many in the society possess the same weakness in some measure or other. No scientific achievement or progress can root out these evils, without a parallel effort on the humane side by each individual.

We as individuals have to take and face the challenge.

CHAPTER 3

Take the Challenge to Rise Above the Animal Passions

The first challenge for each man is therefore to channelise his mind through his will-power, away from the thirteen evil tendencies into *SraddhA and bhakti*. This task is the task of every member of society. If each individual succeeds in the task of minimising, if not eradicating, the thirteen evils inherent in him, the society is automatically on the road to improvement. Not only does this help us to root out the evil tendencies in us but it does much more. Dedication and Devotion will give us the courage not to bend down or kneel before the Gods of corruption, hypocrisy, exploitation, superstition and all the other evils listed above. And this will boost up the morale of the society on its road to progress.

If the individual does not embark upon this task it only means that he has not risen from his animal status. Animals believe in only what is available to their senses. In other words they believe only in the pratyaksha – what is sensed.

paSyanti iti paSavaH

– that is the derivation for the word *paSu*, meaning 'animal'. Only Man can go beyond the senses and think of the unseen, unheard, unsensed. God warns Man by turning his hairs grey and telling him it is time he turns to Him. Note that animals do not develop grey hairs. They behave like what they should, all the time. Only man does not behave like man; he needs the warning and he gets it. That is the latest time, in his life, by which he should turn his devotion and dedication towards nobler goals and purposes. Man certainly takes care of himself, makes his life comfortable, provides amusement for his emotional needs, creates arts and literature for his intellectual needs – these make him different from an animal alright, but he also has an utter disregard for his individual spirituality. When he departs from his own dharma he creates imbalance and perturbation in his own self as well as in his environment. Thereby his progress up the spiritual ladder is impaired; deadly sins are allowed to grow in his heart. He goes down in the scale of *samsAra*, the eternal cycle of births and deaths, in spite of all his secular achievments. What is condemned here is sin and not the sinner. In this sense Hinduism differs from other religions which give man only one birth to do it well or not. <u>Man is not punished *for* his sins; he is punished *by* his sins.</u> Sin is a self-condemning act arising out of a misunderstanding in the sinner as to his own true nature. The going-down in the scale of *samsAra* may mean that one is born in spiritually poorer and more difficult circumstances or one is born even as an animal. But this rebirth takes account of only a small part of our accumulated karma, the conglomerate of our actions and thoughts. There is a large part of our accumulated karma which is the one which contributes to our tendencies and nature in our future births. This can be reshaped by our present actions and thoughts and so it is up to us to act and feel in such a way that our karma opens up a better future for us, if not in this life, certainly in our future lives.

The better future does not simply refer to the spiritual future; it also refers to the material future. Hindu thought and tradition do not undervalue the need for material happiness. It is a mistaken belief to think that Hindu religion emphasizes only asceticism. It wants you to go up the spiritual ladder at your own pace, taste and capacity. It all depends on what you want and how you want it. Do you want earthly pleasures – material goods, sex, wealth, fame, power? Well, you can pursue them all. These goals are termed *artha* (material happiness, wealth) and *kAma* (sensual pleasures). In fact there are four different types of goals which are all legitimate. Technically these are called, *purushArthas* (= man's goals). Besides the two just mentioned, they are: *dharma and moksha.* We gave a meaning to dharma at the top of this page but we shall revert to the various connotations of dharma more than once in this book in a spiral fashion, every time shedding a little more light on the concept. The word *moksha* means salvation or more precisely, liberation.

According to Hinduism, there is nothing wrong in pursuing one or more of these objectives. But Hinduism also asserts with the full force of all its legends, mythology and experience, that in the long run, in due course of everlasting time, that is, if not in this life, in succeeding lives, – really ultimately, one will get tired of pursuing the first three goals (*artha, kAma and dharma*) because frustration is inherent in their pursuit. Experience from time immemorial has left traditions of stories and records which go to show that sooner or later every human being reaches a saturation point in terms of worldly pleasures and wealth, beyond which they breed a frustration syndrome. Everyone wants an ultimate peace-cum-happiness. Pursuit of wealth and happiness are certainly part of our daily lives. The pursuit of dharma relates to moral and social behaviour. This is also, in some sense, in the same ball-park as the other two. Hinduism says that there is a fourth worthwhile goal which is the only goal as far as real ultimate peace-cum-happiness is concerned. And since it believes so, it makes rules even for the pursuit of the other three so that ultimately there is no discordance. In fact in mentioning the four goals of life, Hinduism has a certain sequential order; first it is dharma, next *artha*, then *kAma* and then moksha. In other words, dharma is primary; and so the pursuit of *artha* and *kAma* has to follow the norms of dharma! So the pursuit of even the earthly objectives are to be monitored by rules which are enunciated from the point of view of preparing one to go to the fourth objective, moksha. The idea is, that, when the time comes to seek this fourth goal, beyond the three objectives, either in this life or in later lives, the habits and tendencies accumulated by the ceaseless pursuit of the first three should not come in the way of the fourth. The accumulated habits and tendencies are called *vAsanAs*. (See page 18) The word *vAsanA*, means literally, smell. Technically this is the tendency that we bring along with us from our actions and thoughts of the past like the breeze of air that carries the smell of the rose garden that it has passed through. The animal passions of man have their roots in these *vAsanAs*.

The belief that material happiness is transient does not require a Hindu to neglect the earning of a livelihood or the working of his way up the ladder of worldly success. Far from it. Hinduism has the realism to declare that without a healthy body no spiritual pursuit is possible. Nor can a spiritual seeker sustain himself physically without depending on the environment of a prosperous society. When the Hindu scriptures say that worldly happiness is not the ultimate in happiness they are only reminding us that as we alternate between pleasure and pain, happiness and misery, joy and sorrow, we are only passing from one experience to another – none of which is everlasting. Hinduism pleads with us to stand back and observe ourselves as well as the rest of the world carefully as a scientist. What really is pleasure? It is after all, an intermediate experience between two moments of pain and vice versa. This is not a cynical observation but a ruthless analysis of facts. The two extreme physical experiences of men are birth and death. The first experience leaves no memory and the second experience leaves no experiencer to recall it. In the interval between the two man undergoes an infinite variety of experiences, on the physical, mental and subconscious levels but none of the experiences can be claimed to be permanent. The Upanishads claim on the other hand that Real Permanent Bliss comes from within one's self and that such a bliss which comes from the awareness of one's self is eternal and universal. It requires either a deep intellectual analysis of the self or an actual intuitive experience to corroborate this. It is in the context of such an analysis that one often finds in the scriptures the maxim that material happiness and misery are impermanent and both 'come and go'. All mundane experience of the senses, mind or intellect, whether pleasant or painful are summed up as 'that which comes and goes' (*AgamApAyI*, in Sanskrit) that is, are transient. So one just bears with this syndrome. The fundamental theme of the Hindu teaching, in fact, goes deeper than this. It says: 'What has a beginning must have an end'. To be born means moving towards death. The three goals of man, *dharma, artha and kAma*, all operate only within this cycle of births and deaths. The only thing that transcends this cycle is the status of moksha.

CHAPTER 4

Three Fundamental Urges of Man

To exist, to know and to enjoy – these are the three fundamental urges of man. In fact, all of man's desires, ambitions, aspirations and efforts are based on one or more of these fundamental motives. Certainly the most fundamental urge or instinct is, to be, to survive, to persist (as a being), to perpetuate oneself, to be ever present. It is not relevant to say that not everybody succeeds in this. The fact of this universal urge cannot be gainsaid. It is the urge that is systematically and meticulously sustained by the mother or the mother symbol. The second urge is to enquire, to understand, to investigate, to know and be all-knowing. No one can escape this urge though it may not manifest itself with the same intensity in all people. This urge is sustained, monitored and nurtured by the father (or the father symbol) who introduces one to the external world. The third urge is to enjoy, to be happy, to relax, to experience a satisfactory state. This is common to all human beings; in fact, in some of us it may go even to the extent of expressing itself as an urge to be perfect. Unlike the other two urges one does not find a motivator for this until one discovers one's spouse. It is the spouse who, in the long run, nurtures and monitors the urge to be happy and to enjoy. It is the spouse who shares all the happiness and thereby doubles it and who shares also all the unhappiness and thereby halves it.

Each of these has an infinite expression. The first one expresses itself as the Truth which is the Ultimate. It is the One which survives everything else. In Sanskrit it it is known as *sat*. It is imperishable. It is the immutable anvil that remains the same whatever happens around, on, in, over, or beyond. It is the spark of everything that is animate or inanimate. It may be called, technically, the Spark of Immanence, because it is the Life of all Life, the Soul of all Souls. The infinite expression of the urge to know is Consciousness itself, infinite Intelligence. It is called *cit*. It is neither Knowledge alone, nor the Knower alone, nor the Known alone. It is all three in one. It is an indivisible triad. It is the ultimate Truth which lies beyond all knowledge as the Knower and beside whom everything else becomes the Object. It is always the Subject, which cannot be 'known' in the ordinary sense of the word. The infinite expression of the third urge, namely to be happy and to be perfect is *Ananda*, the eternal bliss. It is the eternal truth from which every spark of enjoyment and experience emanates.

These three urges form the fountainhead for every aspiration of man and its expression in terms of his behaviour and action. Whatever he does in this world is a consequence, direct or indirect, of one or more of these urges. He goes to school because he wants to know, he wants to earn a living by which he can live and, in due time, relax. He marries because he wants to lead a happy life with all its enjoyments. And so on. But all these three urges are just a finite limited version of their corresponding infinite versions, which are called the *sat, cit and Ananda*. This *sat-cid-Ananda* is the ultimate in any experience. It is called the Absolute Reality or the Transcendental Ultimate by Hindu Vedanta. Religion calls it God and gives it several familiar names. Almost right in the beginning of the Gita, the Lord refers to this as the indweller of the body (*sharIrI*) and gives it three connotations of Infinity: namely, *nitya* (eternal), *anAshI* (endless) and *aprameya* (immeasurable). This is how it differs from the Finite which is familiar to our experience. It is eternal whereas anything that is finite is not; it is endless whereas the finite has always an end; and, finally, the infinite is immeasurable or uncountable whereas everything that is finite is either measurable or countable. And the Lord when referring to this Infinite Transcendental Absolute, indicates it as sat, chit, Ananda facets in three different contexts. The first comes out almost right at the beginning of the exposition. What is not can never be; What is can never not be (B.G. II – 16).

na asato vidyate bhAvo na abhAvo vidyate sataH

He confirms it again in B.G.X –20: I am the beginning, the middle and the end of all beings.

aham AdiSca madhyam ca bhUtAnAm anta eva ca

He hints at the cit aspect of His Personality in B.G.II – 46: The One who has known brahman, to him all these vedas and other knowledge are just like a cupful of water before an ocean.

yAvan artha udapAne sarvatas-samplutodake /

tAvAn sarveshu vedeshu brAhmaNasya vijAnataH //

The Ananda aspect comes out in His declaration: Arjuna, I have nothing to do or get done in the three worlds in this life; I have nothing to obtain which I have not obtained … (B.G.III – 22)

na me pArtha asti kartavyam trishu lokeshu kimca na /

na anavAptam avAptavyam … //

thereby implying that his bliss or satisfaction is full.

The advaita Vedanta has this to say on *sat-cid-Ananda*. When a man wakes from deep sleep it is natural for him to exclaim: I slept happily. Who is this 'I' that slept happily? It is not the mind, because it was not active at the time when the 'I' was sleeping. It is not the one that recalls the happiness of the sleep, because it did not experience the happiness. Only the experiencer can recall the experience. The experiencer is the 'I'. Actually the experiencer is the lower 'I', the false 'I'. The real 'I', i.e., the higher

'I', simply watches the experience of the lower 'I'. The real 'I' is the Immutable Reality. It does not go through any change or experience. But it always 'watches'. It is the '*sAkshi*'. It is the *sat-cid-Ananda* Reality. The lower 'I' goes and 'touches' it, as it were, during deep sleep and this is an everyday experience for the lower 'I'. That is why it is able to say 'I slept happily', after every awakening from deep sleep. Here there are three assertions made, all rolled into one. The word 'happily' indicates there is an Ananda (pleasure, happiness, joy) which was experienced during sleep; it is actually a recall of the association with the Ananda of the real 'I'. The word 'I' indicates the continuity of existence between the state of sleep and the state of waking. The word 'slept' indicates an awareness or the knowledge (= *cit*) of sleep, the awareness belonging to the witness to the sleep, namely, the real 'I'. In dreamless sleep were we conscious or not.? We feel we were not conscious. But that is a feeling we have after waking from sleep. We do not do so in sleep itself. That in us which now feels that in sleep we were not conscious is our mind. It was not present in our sleep and so it is natural for it to be ignorant of the consciousness there was in sleep. Not having experienced sleep it is unable to remember what it was like and makes mistakes about it. The state of deep sleep is beyond the mind. Consciousness was present then as consciousness. It is because of that consciousness we are able to say that we were not aware of anything then. In a dark room we are not able to see anything but still we have the awareness that we are not able to see anything; for this awareness no external light is necessary.

This three-fold presentation of Reality, as *sat, cit* and *Ananda* is also reflected in the most important mantra of Hinduism, namely, the *gAyatrI*. The three lines of the *gAyatrI* mean, literally:

That – of the Originator – Most excellent;

Light – of God – Let us meditate;

Intellects – He who – Our – May prompt.

The use of the word *savituh* (= of the Originator) in the first line indicates that He is the Origin of everything in this world. This suggestion of Creation is symbolic of the *sat* face of the Reality. This line is a glorification of the Absolute. The use of the words *dhiyah* (= intellects) and *pracodayAt* (= may prompt or guide) in the third line show that this line is indicative of the *cit* facet of Reality. This line is the prayer imbedded in the *gAyatri*. The second line asks us to meditate as if it is the be-all and end-all of life. Yes, because the meditation itself gives the bliss, immanent in the Absolute Reality. Meditation on the Absolute is communion with or worship of, the Divine. So this line stands for the *Ananda* of the Reality. The three lines together, of the *gAyatrI* incorporate, in a sense, the three-fold universal practice of all Religion, namely,

Glorification of the super-natural, Worship of the Supra-mental and Prayer to The All-mighty.

Can the Finite reach the Infinite? Vedanta says it can. The Infinite which is *sat-cidAnanda* can be reached by the finite human being if proper efforts are made by him. To reach the Infinite is the goal of all beings according to the scriptures. This is the goal referred to as moksha. Once the finite reaches the Infinite, there is no coming back to the finite state. In other words, there is no more birth and death. This reaching the Infinite has to be effected through a proper discipline of the mind. That which IS, by its very nature, is beyond time. Thinking by the mind by its very nature involves a sequence of points in time. Therefore thinking is finite and awareness sparked by this thinking is only of finite objects. It means therefore that in order to contact the infinite, one must go beyond the thought process. That which is, has then to be taken hold of only by the non-action of the thinking function. The mind must be emptied of all its contents in order that its true nature – awareness – may be revealed. At present it is always entangled with some thought so that awareness by itself is lost in that thought. The self disappears in that ego-thought and the outer 'I' mistakes the object for the subject – irrespective of whether the object be the world outside or the thought inside. Thus the mind is the villain within oneself. The most villainous part of the mind is however, the ego. This is the source of all problems. In every one of our actions and thoughts, we have to watch this ego. We have to fight it to minimise its influence. In fact we have to carry on this internal struggle endlessly. This is the Way. The vast majority of people may think of another way or in a variety of other ways. But history has shown us again and again that the mass mind is very amenable to suggestion and regimentation, and can be influenced by appeals to lower instincts, narrow prejudices and baser instincts. It is this mass mind that has made religion a formal affair, a matter of routine and elaborate paraphernalia. Instead of experience, spirituality and love, the mass mind is blinded by dogmatic belief, scholastic learning and charitable work, respectively and mistakes the latter for the former. Our material uplift and the scientific and socio-economic efforts to improve it further is only making us more and more outward looking, superficial and cut off from the only source of strength, peace and wisdom which exists in every one of us. These limitations and illusions of the mind have to be cast off. Only in the innermost depths of our consciousness can we realise the whole Truth in all its Perfection, Immanence and Transcendence. The real life of man begins only when he transcends all his animal attributes and capacities, desires, emotions, concrete thoughts and physical needs and starts living in this (his own) higher level of being.

There is no other Way, declare the scriptures.

'na anyah panthA ayanAya vidyate'

– meaning, to reach salvation there is no other way. Constant chanting of the *gAyatrI*, in the manner of a disciplined *japa* and continuous meditation on its meaning will clear the way for us by consuming the accumulated dirt in our minds. This cleansing of the mind will result in a crystal-clear mind, by the Grace of God, and in that mind one can see the spotless reflection of the Almighty Supreme, say the Seers. This is the way the Finite may reach the Infinite and then there exists only the Infinite; never more the Finite

CHAPTER 5

Empire of the Mind

Man versus Mind:

Mind is the meeting point of science, religion and philosophy. It is the human mind that understands scientific phenomena of nature and coordinates with nature to work out man's 'conquests' of natural phenomena. It is in Man's mind that religion is born, when he needs internal solace and satisfaction. It is with the same mind that man is able to abstract the concrete world before him and go into speculations of philosophy. But with all this it is the mind itself that is man's powerful enemy,

mana eva manuShyANAM sharIrastho mahAripuH'

from Manu-smRRiti

because Man can never say with finality that he is in control of his mind. Hindu Vedanta therefore, placing a great emphasis on the need to control the ind, dwells repeatedly on efforts and strategies for controlling it, even partially. Any effort made in this direction, says the Gita, saves one from great disaster.

svalpam-apyasya dharmasya trAyate mahato bhayAt'

B.G. II – 40

Intellect versus Ego:

Mind is made up of four constituents:

The first is the receiving mind, which receives all impulses and impacts from the external world. It just receives, like an antenna.

What sifts these pieces of information and analyses them is the *buddhi,* the intellect. It is the discerning function of the mind.

There is cittaM, the storage part of the mind,

The agent of all these activities is the *ahamkAra* part of the mind, which by its very nature possesses authority over all actions of the other parts of the mind and therefore constitutes the EGO of man.

These four parts are together called the mind, very often in the literature, without care being taken to distinguish the different functions. The physical framework through which all of them work is of course the brain. But just as the body is the physical basis for the soul which is a subtle entity 'residing' in it, so also the brain is only a physical basis for the mind. Mind is too subtle to be put into any physical framework. But the mind has a power, just as Godhead has a power which is generally called Shakti. This power of the mind is mostly the power of the intellect to decide on a course of action, to fight within itself its own pulls and pushes, mostly prompted, influenced and monitored by the other part of the mind, viz., *ahamkAra*. This power is Will-power. It is the power of the will of Man.

Will versus Fate:

At a crucial point in the discourse of the Bhagavat-Gita, Arjuna wails, (cf. VI – 34): 'Restless indeed is the mind, O Krishna; it is vehement, strong and unconquerable; I deem it as hard to control as the wind'.

CanchalamM hi manaH krishna pramAthi balavad-dRRiDhaM /tasyAhaM nigrahaM manye vAyoriva suduShkaraM //

Arjuna has spoken for all of us. And Krishna replies: Yes, the mind is restless and difficult to restrain. But says He, it may be controlled by constant practice (= *abhyAsa*) and dispassion (= *vairAgya*). (VI – 35):

asamshayam mahAbAho mano durnigrahaM chalaM /abhyAsena tu kaunteya vairAgyeNa ca gRRihyate //

The Will of man must be made more supreme than the mind. Everywhere in the Upanishads the ultimate appeal is to the will and not to the intellect. They would have us not only understand, but do, that is, realize God. This requires an action by one's own will, to start making the effort. The sensations, thoughts, images and facies are all in the mind; but if the will-power is exercised properly with discrimination, all of them can be monitored and channelised. It is not as if man is a helpless creature as a leaf in the storm or a feather in the wind. Man's will has an element of complete freedom. It is the power which enables him to act in directions opposite to his spontaneous tendencies (*VasanAs*). In other words, he can pilot the ship of his personality against his accumulated character and thus control his own future. In this sense Man is the architect of his own fate. Inevitably and ultimately man's will must prove stronger than fate, because it is his own past will which created his present fate.

Restraint versus Resistance

It is not enough to just observe the mind in its normal planes of consciousness. Our will-power is capable of controlling the pulls of the sub-conscious mind also. The normal mind must be taught to restrain (through the intellect) its own vagaries, with the aim of gaining supreme mastery over itself and of ultimately rising above itself to the superconscious state. The villain of the piece is of course the *ahamkaara* part of the mind.

There is a general misconception that control of the mind, exercise of dispassion etc. are austere and forbidding.

It is not so. There is a certain joy and freedom in all these disciplines. The more we master our lower instincts the more we will find ourselves lions of happiness. There is a resistance, no doubt, by the mind. In fact, this resistance itself is nothing but will. To meet this is a challenge, indeed, the challenge. It is necessary to take the challenge at some point of time, if not in this life, in one of our human lives. The sooner the challenge is met, the better, for the spiritual journey of the soul.

To thus change oneself, one has to look at oneself, observe and experiment. This is what is called enquiry followed by practice. That this is possible is what has been taught by all the great spiritual and religious teachers of the world. All self-help books dwell on this in great detail. We shall look at it in the context of religion, particularly, Hinduism.

Do it yourself

The mind is certainly meshed up with all other components of the self, like *ahamkaara* but fortunately the mind itself has the capacity and the role to take the lead in changing the lower self into the higher self. By overcoming desire, vanity, violence and untruth, by its own efforts, the normal mind with discretion as master, and an exercise of will-power, can train the lower self to rise above its barbarian nature and rise in spirituality. Purity of mind is nothing but the state of being filled with divine consciousness. This is where Vedanta helps us to approach the problems of life with clarity and firmness. It helps us loosen our spiritual ignorance and ultimately destroy it. This is what exactly the word *'upanishat'* stands for.

CHAPTER 6

Miracles, Wonders and Prayers

Miracles are one aspect of religion – and there are so many of them in every religion – which the rational mind rebels against. In fact, more often than not, any discussion of Science and Spirituality is likely to end up into a debate on miracles. If you probe carefully into someone who is disinclined towards spirituality and if you scratch below the surface you will find that the real reason is disbelief of what is usually called a miracle and a consequent distaste for anything that is termed supernatural. The concept of *avatAra* (divine descent or manifestation) – so special to Hinduism – is another part of the miracle story which drives away the skeptic. That God can descend to the earthly level of manifestation, live amongst us like one of us, eat and drink like all of us, beats the imagination of a 'scientific' mind. But this is where one may see the other side of Man. In addition to the scientific-rational side of the human personality each human being has also a 'super-natural' or extra-sensory side. Many would not accept this until they have the experience themselves. This is where Hinduism has a contributing factor. The entire atmosphere is full of such anecdotes and histories. Each family has experience to narrate.

Modern minds may ascribe all this to mere superstition and naivete. But try visiting one of the famous retreats or residences of great Acharyas and religious leaders. Listen to the personal stories of the people present there, - not necessarily permanently, but who are visiting just like you. Listen to how each was not a 'believer' once and how the same person was later 'converted' by an inexplicable force. Throw away the frills and exaggerations which the person is likely to make because of his close involvement with the story. Finally one would come out with a feeling of daze, awe and reverence. The moral of all this is: <u>Have the will to suspend your disbelief.</u> Try to gather as much information as you like from those who have had the experience. Then come to your own conclusions.

The most well-known divine descents in Hindu tradition are those of Rama and Krishna. But each such descent has its own purpose and its own natural style of behaviour and teachings Throughout his life Rama never declares himself as an *avatAra* though the sages of His time believed Him to be so. He behaves like an ordinary mortal but exhibits extraordinary human qualities and lives the life of an ideal person. On the other hand the *avatAra* of Krishna loses no time in declaring Himself to be God on earth. In fact He announces it to the father and mother of the child- to-be-born in the most dramatic way, as a producer of a play would introduce the Director of the play. He performs miracle after miracle, almost for the asking.

His life is full of apparent contradictions and only the really blessed ones in his lifetime recognize him as the manifestation of the supreme. Coming to our own times we have it on the authority of the personal experiences of several devotees that fully evolved beings like Ramakrishna, Aurobindo, Ramana Maharshi, Kanchi Maha-swamigal and Sathya Sai Baba cannot but be manifestations of the Supreme Divinity.

The natural questions that usually arise in the mind of a modern rational human being are many. Some of them could be the following:

If all these are *avatAras* of Divinity why have all the problems of the suffering world not been solved? Why are people still suffering? If God has come down on earth why is He allowing suffering to continue? Why do we fight right before his eyes? Having manifested on earth, why does'nt He solve our problems?

These questions certainly rise, at one time or another, in all thinking minds who are eager to understand Divinity and its purpose. But we forget we think of these questions only in relevance to an *avatAra*. Why is it the same questions are not asked in respect of that all-knowing omnipresent Divinity irrespective of whether He comes down on earth as a manifestation or not? Even when Divinity is in its own heaven, surely it is aware of all the sufferings man is subject to. So why does it not remove our sufferings by a stroke of its magic power? Thus posed the question looks childish.

So then, what is the purpose of a descent of Divinity on earth? It is only to establish faith in the existence of a higher Reality and the truth of spiritual laws, so that man may have the strength to turn towards righteousness and steadfastly work for salvation of himself and his contemporaries. If the Supreme Reality in the form of either the Omnipresent Divinity or an *avatAra* solved all our problems of poverty and disease, would that be the end of our problems? No. The cure of our bodily illnesses or of our poverty would still leave us spiritually as we were, at the same level of consciousness and spiritual evolution as before, so that very soon we would be at one another's throats. The same chaotic world will continue. A God can perhaps convert the entire ocean water, or at least a large part of it, into oil, so that the fuel problems of the world can be solved immediately, but even God cannot give a guarantee that no crazy man would throw a lighted cigarette in that sea of oil, because man has the free will to do so. If God had really a purpose in descending on earth, it would be only to clear the way for our spiritual growth! People who have been around the God-men of the 20th century, who are known to perform 'miracles' are of the opinion that they are personally experiencing the even more unbelievable miracle of transformation that is taking place within themselves - and they are seeing and feeling and hearing of the countless, deep personal transformations occuring within the throngs of people at the ashram and around the world. Many come to observe the miracles and stay on to experience the great personal growth that accrues to those who come. The miracles force an expansion of consciousness: it is like opening the gates in our scientific stalls and being invited to gallop out beyond our limits. We are reminded that we need to shift our beliefs, that there is more to this life than we think we know.

One may wonder why we are not asking the question: If God exists and did create the universe what was His purpose in such a creation? In fact this is an important question which occupies the mind of every scientist who investigates into the frontiers of science leading him into questions of spirituality and God. The MuNDaka-Upanishad answers this question by citing three analogies for the relationship between the universe and the Godhead, Brahman, which is the origin of the universe according to the Upanishads. The three analogies are contained in the verse: *MuNDaka-Upanishad, I - 1 - 7:*

yathorNanAbhiH sRRijate gRRihNate ca

yathA pRRithivyAM oshhadhayaH sambhavanti.

yathA sataH purushhAt kleshalomAni tathA.
akshharAt sambhavatIha vishvam..

Meaning: Just as the spider emits its own saliva to build its web and withdraw it;

just as plants grow on earth naturally without any effort

just as hairs grow on a man spontaneously,

so also the universe emanates from the Imperishable brahman.

The first analogy raises the doubt that the Ultimate may have a purpose, like the spider. No, says the second analogy. But the latter raises another objection questioning whether brahman, the Ultimate, is unconscious or inert like the Earth. To answer this, look at the third analogy. Hair grows on a man without effort or strain, so does the universe sprout from brahman, just as an extraneous projection of His shakti or *prakRti*.

The most complete incarnation of God in Hinduism is supposed to be the descent of Krishna. The most comprehensive popular scripture in Hinduism is the Mahabharata. The most-often quoted Hindu scripture is the Bhagavad-Gita. That these three together encompass a large part of the mythology, literature and philosophy of Hinduism is surely well-known. But what is not usually noticed is their subtle mutual dependence. It is as if the Gita and the Mahabharata were made for each other. Without Krishna as the Director-cum-actor the story of the Mahabharata would have been just a family feud long forgotten. Without the backdrop of the Mahabharata story the Gita would have lost all its contextual reference and would have been just one more wave in the ocean of Upanishads. Without the culmination in the divine exposition at the most crucial point in the story, the story of the epic would not have reached epic proportions. Over and above all this is the importance of two great supernatural events without which none of the three would be what they are today in the Hindu milieu. One is the critical scene in Dritarashtra's assembly where the entire bunch of great men of the times, each great in his own way, had to remain dumb witnesses to the worst-ever downfall of dharma and also to the most miraculous protection of the princess's honor that came from the only Savior of dharma, the living divinity of that age. The other event is the unfolding of the Universal cosmic Form of the Lord on the battlefield, without which the Gita itself would have missed all its spiritual sanction. The Mahabharata without the miraculous scene of the protection of the honor of Draupadi would just be some dry history and the Gita without its wonderful eleventh chapter, called the Yoga of the showing of the Cosmic form, would be just a lifeless lecture on the subtleties of individual, social and political ethics. These two miracles may therefore be considered as of great fundamental value.

A philosopher or an intellectual may rise by successive steps of reasoning to the level of understanding an unchanging Atman which is omnipresent, omnipotent and omniscient. A true devotee also is ready to grant that there is a Supreme Power who controls everything. But the vast majority of people are neither philosophers nor intellectuals nor are they convinced devotees of the Lord. They believe in God only when that God expresses Himself through miracle-healing or through inexplicable phenomena. It is a moot point whether Jesus or Krishna would be held in as much esteem as they are today if their stories were totally devoid of miracles! But what we consider to be miracles are not miracles for Divinity. From the viewpoint of Divinity what appears to be a miracle for us is just a normal expression of the infinite love with which Divinity always overflows. The human mind as a single isolated factor is a microcosmic and insignificant speck in the vastness of total experience and it cannot in that isolated state understand the subtlety of religious spirituality, much less solve a single problem of either itself or of humanity.

The value of prayer can never be overstated. The so-called fate cannot. No one can reveal God to another. But by revealing the value of prayer and inculcating the habit of prayer we place ourselves in a position to receive God-experience, in due time. Spiritual experience can come only through the correct understanding of prayer. Prayer is the point of contact with God. Silent prayer is the preparation of consciousness for the experience of Divinity within. We should tune ourselves from childhood well enough so that at adult age we are ready to receive the inevitable message that unhappiness and suffering are necessary for the unfolding of the soul within and to stand that unhappiness and suffering, prayer is the nutrition needed. From the age of 5, the practice of silent prayer should become a daily routine for a child irrespective of the denomination or religion to which the child belongs or does not belong. The habit of prayer must be made a second nature. This should not be left for the child to learn by itself after it reaches adult age – as is the experience of many a materialist adult who has learnt things the hard way and then, turned to the ways of the Orient in the past few decades. This is where it is not possible to accept the plea of the rationalist that, to pray or not to pray should be left to the individual for a decision on his own, when he becomes an adult. The plea assumes that each man, without standing on the shoulders of the men of earlier times, begins all over again to learn all that the earlier civilization has already discovered and recorded for us to take the torch from there. That is not the way Man has ascended to the present state of knowledge.

CHAPTER 7

Jiva, Atman and Soul

IMPORTANT NOTE: For a beginner this chapter could be the most difficult chapter to digest, It is also the core content of Advaita vedAnta,, Learners should read slowly several times back and forth to understand and assimilate. To boot, get a knowledgeable person (in Vedanta) near you to help you!

Jiva, Atman & Soul ! — Are they not the same? They are not. That is exactly the problem. This is part of the topic of this chapter

These three words, are very often used by some readers and authors of messages or articles on spirituality, without the mathematical precision needed to distinguish them. Let us try our best to sort this out.

In fact we shall not dwell specifically upon the word 'soul' at all. We shall dwell on the word JIva elaborately and as we go on it will be clear that the English word 'soul' (whatever meaning it has) does not have the connotations that 'JIva' has. Left to myself I would not use the word 'soul' at all – though I have myself slipped in my books (including this book!)

Samsara is a great time process in which every living being is involved. The state of each creature in a particular life is preconditioned by the good and bad thoughts and actions of its previous lives. This very idea is based on the fundamental maxim of Sanatana Dharma that each individual JIva travels from body to body. At this point, take the JIva to mean 'the embodied Atman' or the empirical Self. What is individualized in this fashion is the conglomerate of the mind with all its 'impressions' clinging on to the Jiva (not to the Self or the Atman).

There is an Imperishable *Purusha* within us (to be shortened as IP in this article; The Sanskrit word is *akshara-purusha*). *Purusha* may be translated rather meekly as 'Personality'. This *Purusha* is the real 'I' (the Atman). In ordinary conversation when we use the first person pronoun 'I' we mean the conglomeration of the body-mind-intellect which we claim as ours. Except for sages like Ramana Maharishi, very rarely do people distinguish between the real 'I' within and the common 'transactional' I. The real I, namely the IP within us does not do any action, does not think any thoughts, does not feel any emotions. He is unaffected, unperturbed, uncontaminated, unsullied by any of the happenings to the PP (Perishable purusha which is the *JIva*). The IP is the One introduced by Krishna very early in the Gita in verses 23, 24, 25 of the 2nd chapter (*nainam chindanti, achhedyoyam, avyktoyam*) and later, in many other contexts. IP, being the real 'I', can therefore very well say: "I am not the doer or the experiencer" – like the street light that witnesses everything that happens under the light but is itself neither the doer nor the experiencer of the happenings, –

He is the non-participating witness to everything that happens to the PP. At the final end of the theory of non-duality one is told that the knower, the known and the knowledge are all one. But, ordinarily, the knower is the subject and the known is the object. The subject which knows the object is the centre of consciousness. It exists, and it knows. The object only exists and even that, only as a transactional reality.

The *JIva* (the PP) is the subject of all experience. It is a complex of Consciousness (ChaitanyaM) and Matter. When objects are in relation to the subject we have the stream of presentations called *vrittis*. When there are no objects there will be no presentations but the consciousness that lights up the presentations will remain. That consciousness is the Witness, the non-participating Witness. Objects are not presented to Consciousness as such. They are directly presented to the JIva and only indirectly to the Witness. There can be no relationship between Consciousness and objects, because they belong to different orders of reality, like the rope and the snake. The subject, the centre of consciousness, is experienced directly in an intuition, like an 'I-feeling' (*aham-pratyaya*), but the object is known only from the outside like 'this-feeling' (*idam-pratyaya*).

Then how did this Pure Consciousness become the JIva or the empirical self and how was the JIva made the subject of all experience? Strictly speaking, there is no 'becoming, no making, no transition, no transformation'. Pure Consciousness (Atman, Brahman) does not undergo any change of form or character. JIva is only Brahman in an empirical dress of BMI in which the sprouting of the thought of distinctness from Brahman has occurred.(God knows when! Neither the Vedas nor the Upanishads say when this occurred! They say it is *anAdi*, beginningless). This thought of individuality is the Ego, the starting point of the JIva. **JIva is therefore Consciousness conditioned by Ignorance in the form of an ego of individuality**. The Self can have no direct knowledge of the world except through the apparatus of the BMI. This apparatus as well as the small world which becomes the object of its knowledge is spoken of as the adjunct (*upAdhi*) of Consciousness. All this adjunct is matter. Consciousness ('*Chaitanyam*') which has this limited portion of matter for its adjunct is the JIva. Each JIva has its own knowing apparatus and moves in a small world of its own, with its own joys and sorrows and thus has its own individual existence. Though the Self is one, the JIvas are many.

Shankara draws attention to this fact of one Self and several JIvas, for instance, in his commentary on

B.G.2-12 where the Lord says There was never a time when I was not there nor you were not there, nor these leaders of men nor that we, all of us, will come to be hereafter. He comments: 'The plural number (in we) is used following the diversity of the bodies, but not in the sense of the multiplicity of the Self'. Generally in his commentaries, Shankara uses two illustrations to bring home this point. <u>One is the sun appearing as many reflected images in different pools of water.</u> If the waters are dried up the several images get back to the original sun. <u>The other illustration is the infinite space being delimited by artificial barriers.</u> If these barriers are knocked down there will be no occasion to speak of the different spaces. These two illustrations of the exact mode of conceiving the relation between the Self and the JIva gave rise to two schools of argument in later advaita, namely,

the argument of original and its reflection

(*bimba-pratibimba-vAda*),

and the argument of delimitation

(*avaccheda-vAda*).

The former is the *VivaraNa* school and the latter is the *BhAmati* school. Thus when Consciousness is conditioned by its association with Ignorance or Matter it is no longer Pure Consciousness but a complex of both, called JIva, This does not mean however that Matter or Ignorance is outside of the Reality of Consciousness, because that would contradict non-duality. The relation between Atman and Jiva has therefore to be conceived in the following way.

The addition of the adjunct is only a difference in the standpoint that we adopt. There are two standpoints – the intuitive and the intellectual. The intuitive is that of immediate and direct realisation. It is the method of the mystics. There is no dualism of subject and object there, nor that of doer and the deed, nor that of agent and enjoyer. These distinctions of duality arise only in the intellectual method of looking at reality. That is why the Gita says that it is "beyond the intellect" (*buddheH param*)(III – 43). It is the nature of the intellect to break up the original unity and revel in these distinctions. At this intellectual level what we are doing is actually a come-down in the level of perception. The JIva is now perceived in relation to its own small world, the subject in relation to the object and the doer in relation to the deed. The Self thus reflected in the medium of the intellect becomes the JIva.

As per the VivaraNa school, the Atman or the Self is the original, the intellect is the reflecting medium and the JIva is the reflected image. In the case of the BhAmati school, the Atman is the infinite space, the adjuncts (upAdhis) are the limiting barriers and the JIvas are the small spaces.

kUTastha: The Immutable or The Immovable; that which remains like the unchanging iron-piece (anvil = *kUTa*) on which the blacksmith does all his hammering. In Vedanta literature *kUTastha* is used to denote the *akshara purusha*, the imperishable Self or the IP (the *Atman*), who is the changeless non-participating witness of the doings of the outer self. The outer Self, which is the PP, is involved in the actions of Nature, reflects the varied workings of the *guNas* of the individual's prakriti (this is just the store of the *Vasanas* of the Jiva earmarked for this birth Shankara is very clear on this. He gives the meaning in his commentary to B.G.3-33. Prakriti that controls an individual, is his Nature, says he, meaning all impressions of work, righteous and unrighteous, done already, which manifest themselves in the present life. PP identifies himself with the play of personality and assumes the doer-ship of all actions. He is under the constant spell of *mAyA* (meaning his own *Prakriti*); whereas the *akshara purusha*, the *kUTastha*, is the inactive non-doer and is only the witnessing Self. It is the Lord that appears as both the *purushas*. The *kUTastha* or the *akshara purusha* is witnessing everything. It is because of this existence of a continuous witness, that the outer Self when it goes to sleep along with its BMI, has however a memory of the sleeping act ('I slept soundly and happily') when it wakes up after sleep. This is a daily phenomenon that happens without our noticing it carefully. In *yajur-veda, taittirIya-AraNyaka, 10 - 1-67* there is a *mantra:*

'aham-eva-aham-mAM-juhomi svAhA',

meaning, 'I make myself (the finite self) an oblation into the fire of the infinite Brahman which I am always'. This mantra, truly enunciates the refunding of the individual self into its source, the Supreme Self, or the realisation of the identity between the *JIva* and the *Ishvara* when the adjuncts created by ignorance are removed (by the oblation of the lower self into the Fire of the Higher Self). The outer Self (PP) goes and 'merges' as it were with the Inner Self (IP) during sleep and that is what makes it conscious of the sleep after the event. *It is this daily event that is the proof of the theory that the kshara purusha and the akshara purusha are essentially the same.* Recall *Kshetrajno-kshhara eva ca* in Vishnu sahasranamam

The JIva is thus a complex of Consciousness (*Chaitanyam*) and matter It is Pure Consciousness with a limited adjunct of matter, namely, the BMI. (In other words, Matter permeated by Spirit). This limited adjunct is spoken of as the Ignorance (*avidyA*) of the JIva. This Ignorance is a colossal age-old Ignorance (as we have already mentioned). It is the wrong (=mistaken) identification by the JIva of itself with whatever is the (external) personality of BMI, in which it currently resides. This is what makes the *JIva* the (individual) PP. That is why the *JIva* suffers and goes through birth after birth. The *JIva* has to learn to identify itself with the IP. When the *JIva* strips itself of its adjunct it loses its individuality and is then nothing but Pure *ChaitanyaM*.

The analysis of the three states of waking, dreaming and sleeping is intended to show that Consciousness is the only constant factor running through them all. Even in the sleeping state, this Consciousness is there. That nothing is seen (made aware of) in that state is because, although seeing then, it does not see; for the vision of the Witness can never be lost, because it is imperishable. But then no second thing exists there separate from it which it can see. (Br. U. IV – 3-23). Shankara quotes this passage in his commentary to Brahma sutra II-3-18 and adds his own explanation: This appearance of absence of awareness is owing to the absence of objects of knowledge, but not owing to the absence of consciousness. It is like the non-manifestation of light, spread over space, owing to the absence of things on which it can be reflected, but not owing to its own absence.It is in the fourth state called 'turIya', that transcends the three states of waking, dream and dreamless sleep, all traces of Ignorance disappear.

When the JIva is thus disassociated from Ignorance and therefore from all material vesture, the spiritual core of the JIva comes into its own. Shankara sets forth (in his commentary on Brahma sutra. I-3-19) the nature of this transcendence of all adjuncts in the following way. A white crystal placed by the side of something red or blue appears red or blue on account of the adjunct. But in reality the crystal is only white. When the adjunct is removed, it does not 'acquire' its white colour but only shines in its own natural colour. Before the onset of true enlightenment the Spirit (Consciousness) on account of its association with the BMI appears as the *JIva*. But the rise of true knowledge does make a real difference. All false notions disappear and Spirit rises to its true stature. The self-hood of the empirical self falls to the ground and the Self shines forth in its original splendour. To know the highest truth is only to know the self in its true nature. The moment true enlightenment dawns on man he realises that he is no other than the non-dual self, that very moment he sheds his finitude and rises to his full stature. <u>There is no question of the JIva merging in anything other than itself. It simply comes to its own.</u>

It is to come into its own, that the individualized Jiva (with all its 'carry-on' baggage of *prArabdha karma* and coating of vAsanas) – a note in a lighter vein: *sancita-karma* is 'checked-in' baggage! – travels from body to body and acquires further experience. If these experiences and doings of the individualized *JIva* are of the *sAtvic* kind (rid of all attachment), slowly, the balance of acquired karma diminishes and, hopefully, ultimately dives to zero. That is when the *JIva* comes into its own, and then there is no more of this individualized *JIva*.

This is where certainly the Hindu concept of *JIva* has to be distinguished from the western concept of 'soul'. The soul of the western philosophies is also individualized, but it does not carry any vAsanAs, nor there is any concept of Vasanas. There is no comparison between the long journey of transmigration of the *JIva* until its own non-existence and the soul's long sojourn of rest in the grave, until it is one day redeemed by the Supreme. That is why, one in the West says RIP (Rest in Peace) for the soul and one in Sanatana Dharma says 'May the *JIva* go to a noble destination, which enables its upward spiritual journey in its future lives' .

In truth, – now this may jolt you; but this is where Advaita Vedanta clean-bowls you! – (from the standpoint of the Absolute Reality), there is no entity as the JIva at all. It is not among the things created. It is a false creation due entirely to adventitious ('*Agantuka*') or incidental circumstance, that is, coming from without and not pertaining to the fundamental nature. "The idea of embodiedness is a result of nescience. Unless it be through the false ignorance of identifying the Self with the body, there can be no embodiedness for the Self"

('*sa-sharIratvasya mithyA-jnAna-niimittatvAt ....*
kalpayituM':

Shankara's Commentary on Br. Su. I-1-4).

JIva has always remained Brahman. Only the adjuncts have to be removed for this truth to stand out. Once this realisation is there, the finitude of the JIva will disappear, as also its misery and its supposed agency and enjoyership. "When that Brahman, the basis of all causes and effects, becomes known, all the results of the seeker's actions become exhausted" (Mu.U. II-2-8). The transmigration of the JIva which is due to its false association with the adjuncts, will also come to a close. That is when the ego-thought of separateness from the Supreme Self, with an 'I' of its own, will get destroyed. That is what we mean by saying 'JIva attains mokSha'. The two things are simultaneous, like the simultaneity of disappearance of darkness with the lighting of a match. But that does not mean that JIva 'obtains something'. '*JIva* sees the Truth' simply means that it sees that it is itself Brahman. In other words, it wakes up to the Truth that was always there. Not waking up to the Truth was the Ignorance. Ignorance is not in Brahman, which is pure and self-illumined, but in the *JIva*. So long however as the latter does not realize his identity with Brahman, ignorance is said, rather loosely (and metaphorically), to envelop Brahman. And that long, will the *JIva* keep transmigrating from body to body, in fact from death to death!

All the injunctions that are given by the Vedas to man are given to him in his state of ignorance because activity is natural to man in that state. The Self is never the doer. The injunction is only a restatement following what is given in experience. All the ritual purifications through chanting of mantras and the results of such actions are enjoined on, and enjoyed by, that entity which has the idea "I am the doer", as stated in the Mundaka Upanishad mantra "One of the two enjoys the fruits having various tastes, while the other looks on without enjoying" (Mu. U. III-1-1). The misery that falls to the lot of the *JIva,* the empirical self, is entirely due to its fancied association with its adjuncts. This association imagines such 'realities' as 'I am a brahmin', 'I am a renunciate', 'I am a JIva' and the like. When the *JIva* sheds these imagined realities and all adventitious adjuncts and realises its true nature by a discrimination between the permanent and the ephemeral, then there is an end of all its misery. Except by such knowledge of the Ultimate Self, misery and finitude cannot be overcome.

While *JIva* is matter permeated by spirit, the concept of Ishvara, the SaguNa brahman, arises when spirit is taken in association with insentient matter, or, what is the same thing, Brahman is viewed through our intellect. The essential content of *JIva* and Ishvara is the same fragment of the consciousness aspect of Brahman. While the para Brahman, the Supeme Absolute Brahman, is without attributes Saguna Brahman is the form of Brahman which we can worship, pay reverence to, adore, serve and pray to. It is the greatness of advaita philosophy that it brings down the attributeless absolute Brahman to the level of ordinary man by means of the 'other form' (*apara-svarUpa*) of Brahman, for purposes of worship as the god of religion and thus synthesizes the apparently conflicting thoughts in the maze of multifold Upanishadic expressions.

TheMahAvAkya 'That Thou Art' states the essential identity of consciousness between *JIva* and Ishvara. Inspite of the difference in their adjuncts, they are identical in so far as their real self is concerned. In the case of the *JIva* it is our own Ignorance (*avidyA)* and thus it is consciousness delimited by avidyA. In the case of Ishvara it is consciousness delimited by Cosmic *AvidyA*, that is *mAyA*. *AvidyA* and *mAyA* are extraneous adjuncts. If the JIva and Ishvara are rid of these there will be nothing to distinguish them from each other or both from Brahman.The analysis of the three states of consciousness is intended to show that it is Brahman, in its fragmentary form of *JIva*-Ishvara, that is the constant factor running through all the three states: the gross, the subtle and the causal – *sthUla, sUkshma* and *kAraNa*. These three are elaborated in Taittiriyopanishad as five *koshas* (sheaths).

The gross body (*annamaya-kosha*) is perishable. The subtle body (consisting of the *prANa-maya, mano-maya*, vijnAna maya koshas) is something like a permanent annexe of the JIva throughout its transmigratory career which comes to an end when it has acquired the knowledge that it is Brahman and has rid itself of the adjunct of Ignorance. Merit and Demerit will have exhausted themselves. The subtle body will then drop off. The causal body (*Ananda-maya kosha*: kAraNa sharIra) will also drop off, because it is nothing but the *vASanA* factor and the store of vAsanAs would have come to nil since no vAsanAs are acquired by an egoless jIva. The *JIva* will then cease to be *jIva* and rise to its true stature as Brahman. This is the glorious consummation towards which each JIva is striving.

CHAPTER 8

On Prakriti

The concept of *prakRti* is most fundamental to the understanding of Indian metaphysics. The nearest English translation of the word *prakRti* is Cosmic Energy, though the innocuous word 'Nature' is very often used by scholars and laymen alike. The difference between the connotation of *prakRti* as used in Vedanta and the meaning of the word Energy as used in Science is actually at the root of the matter. In Science, Matter is fundamental and self-existent; its motive-power is Energy. In Vedanta, Energy is self- existent, and Matter is the product of this ever-present Energy. It is the qualities *(= guNas)* inherent in Cosmic Energy, not as something separate but as the constituents which make up the Cosmic Energy, that gives matter its substance. The qualities are something like strands of the twisted rope of *prakRti*.

There are, as it were, two *prakRti*s, both emanating as the power of Brahman, the Absolute Reality. The inferior *prakRti* (aparA-*prakRti*) is the Energy that gives rise to Matter. This is also called in the literature by its various names: *mAyA*, because it deceptively hides the spirit behind matter and projects falsity;

pradhAna, the most fundamental, because under the will of Ishvara, God, it produces the five elements and then the universe; *avyakta,* the unmanifest, because it is not perceptible to the senses; *jaDa,* the insentient; *avidyA,* cosmic ignorance; *kshara,* the perishable, because it alternates between manifestation and non-manifestation; and *kshetra,* the field, because it is the base of all action.

The Superior *prakRti* contributes to the spark of the spiritual undercurrent vibrating in each living being. It is known as *parA-prakRti,* also *parA-shakti,* the supreme power of brahman, also *cit-shakti,* the power of cognition, or pure consciousness or pure spirit. It is the source of all energy. It is the abstract form of Brahman to be known and realised by intuition. A tiny fragment of it appears as *JIva,* the individual soul, on the one side and Ishvara, God, on the other side. The contrast between *JIva* and Ishvara is as follows:

JIva is matter in association with Spirit under a material envelope and is also under the constant spell of *mAyA.* Ishvara is Spirit viewed in relation to matter. It is Brahman conditioned by our intellect and is in complete control of *mAyA or avidyA.*

Free will is the sheet anchor on which we base all our actions. But that is only the starting point. As we move up the spectrum of spiritual evolution slowly but steadily we reach the stage where we look upward for the hand of God to help us out of our problems, and we believe that God can change things for us. But shall we trust Him totally? Or shall we take it that He gives us just a hand? Many of us go through this dilemma most of our lives vacillating between extremes. The intensity of this vacillation depends on our mood, our environment, the company we keep, the amount of pressure from our peers, kith and kin, the attachment we have to what we think is our objective and what we think is our prerogative, and, finally, the habits we have cultivated for ourselves in terms of our attitude to crises. A trust in God and His omnipotence does not mean that we are demeaning ourselves. Belief in the concept that it is some other Power within us, other than our egoism, that is the doer and the experiencer, should not be equated with fatalism. It is in fact the first step to the import of spirituality in our lives. This other Power within us is usually ascribed to be the Lord but it is actually our own *prakRti*. This latter is usually translated as Cosmic nature but in this context it is nothing but the accumulated *vAsanAs* due to the actions of our past lives individualized and earmarked for this life of ours. (The accumulated actions themselves so individualized and earmarked for this life of ours is *prArabdha-karma* which may be roughly translated as fate). So each person brings a chip of imprints from his previous lives; this is his *prakRti*. Each action of ours is not merely a product of the action or thought that precedes it but it is also the product of a state of moral character which is our own *prakRti*. It is not God's action, except that it is He that is the distributor of results of past deeds. This is the answer to the standard question of the atheist: If you believe in a supernatural interventionist God, how do you explain the non-interventions?

There is another way in which Fate and Free will are mixed up. In one of the *smRtis* (the secondary scriptures) it says that among the four objectives of man, *artha* (material prosperity) and *kAma* (sensual desires) are obtained as per one's *prArabdha* karma while the other two, namely, *dharma* (righteousness) and *moksha* (ultimate release from bondage) are obtained by self-effort. This would imply that as far as these two goals – *dharma* and *moksha* – are concerned, a total freedom is given to us, as is confirmed by the religious injunctions like 'speak the truth' and 'do the right thing'. Self-effort is the most essential ingredient, therefore, for lifting ourselves spiritually.

The concept of free will changes as one evolves philosophically. Fate and free will are interwoven just as the threads of a fabric are crossed and interlaced. We cannot rewrite our past. Our past is our fate for the future. We may not be able to repair our wrong actions, but we can certainly learn lessons from them and act accordingly, by a determined free will, in the future. We may not be able to alleviate the miseries that we have caused others but we may avoid repeating them. It is our tendencies that are determined by the so-called fate and not our actions. Actions are ours. This is the hypothesis from which we all start our lives. But as we go through life we learn some lessons from the world. We become wiser to the ways of the world and also to the ways of the Lord. Slowly it appears that, try as we may, certain happenings which seemed to be totally in our control have slipped away from us and we see an invisible force pulling us. We move from the childhood beliefs of naivete, myth and superstition to the adult days of self-effort and freedom of free will. From this position we have to learn the lessons of philosophy. Gradually and wisely the movement is towards accepting the Supreme as the really supreme mover of things. Real free will is that of the Self within.

The common man's understanding that the Almighty intervenes either by way of grace or otherwise is rather elementary. The real work of the Almighty is deeper. Not a leaf moves without His knowledge or sanction, not a drop flows down by itself. Gravity is His Will. Action and reaction are His Will. This is not poetic fancy or philosophical speculation. This is the basis on which God's omnipotence and omniscience are asserted by the scriptures of Vedanta at the highest levels of understanding. The free will that we usually talk about is not any more free. Mortals as we are, we however think that we are the most significant creatures on this earth. But perhaps a bevy of ants occupying a log of wood floating in the ocean has also a significance. Our entire humanity occupying this planet is itself floating in a limitless universe and will be inevitably swallowed up in empty space and oblivion leaving no trace behind. Man's will, though powerful as we thought, has only a limited power. Will is concerned with ends. Power is concerned with the means for attaining the end. Will without power is helpless to provide the means to attain the end. Power without will is purposeless because it has no end in view. There cannot be any power without consciousness. There cannot be consciousness without power. The will-power we thought was ours comes really from the consciousness within. The free will and the will power are both egoistic, being individual- centered. The true center of all action is not the ego, though it appears to be so, and rightly so, in the beginning. The true center is the free Self within us. The will in us as well as the will in Nature are only a modified and partial reflection of this Will of the Self within us.

QUESTIONS galore: What does it mean to say that the Self or God is free? Does He have free will? Free will implies multiple options and a freedom to exercise choice. Does He have several options? Why does He choose one of them? In that case is He so ignorant of the future to have to choose from his options? What governs His choice? Nature or *prakRti*? Is He a slave to His Nature? What desire makes Him choose? If He is omniscient, omnipotent and omnipresent, why does He have to have options, choices, freedom to choose or not to choose? Why? why? why? Does it not all add up to saying that such a God is a bundle of contradictions?

To answer all these questions one has to dole out a vast material about the concept of Godhead in Hinduism. We shall just briefly give the punch line. Whatever you take the Ultimate Godhead to be, either impersonal or personal, what is important is that the Hindu description of Godhead is rather tricky because it simultaneously possesses "contradictory' qualities. So it is difficult to think of a parallel in the finite world of ours. He has no desire, yet He has Will! He chooses and chooses not! He intervenes and He also never intervenes, only watches! He has options but each option is His own Will! He knows the future, yet He chooses to act! The future is what He makes of the present. Nature (= *prakRti*) is His slave, but He allows Nature to take its course. He is Personal, but not 'personal' in the worldly sense, because He is all- knowing. He is perfect, not in the sense of free from limitations, because limitations don't exist outside of His will! Yes, He is a bundle of contradictions, if you yourself don't have faith in your Self! *PrakRti*, the Nature of each being, is only the force of the Self within. It is this Self within, called the *purusha* that makes the *prakRti* work through the lower self. The Bhagavad-Gita makes an impassioned appeal for us to make this surrender to the Self within. After showing His cosmic form to Arjuna, Krishna declares: I have already conquered and vanquished all your enemies; be only an instrument of my action; go and fight. So the plea is for us to be the instrument of God's Will. We are supposed to be like the needle in a gramophone which only traces the channels already chalked out for it by the designer of the record.

The ascent to this height in spirituality is not easy. To sacrifice the will itself to the divine is a major requirement of deep spirituality. This has to be an effort over a long period of years in one life. Hindu scriptures say that one life may not be sufficient for this. That it takes quite several lives before one reaches this stage is a standard refrain of scriptural advice. The Bhagavad-Gita also says this. And in saying this, the Gita dwells upon why it is so difficult. The mind is made up of soft matter. As each thought or memory of an action passes through it, an impression (like perhaps a scratch) is left on the mind. When similar thoughts are repeated this 'scratch' deepens into a canal. Every subsequent thought wave has a tendency to flow through that ready-made thought canal. Each individual brings with him at birth this particular shade (*vAsanA*) of imprint, in his mind from his previous lives. The shade-mix of the aggregate of *vAsanAs* must be congenial and conducive to the growth of Spirituality. Human behavior is generally attributed to what is usually called one's nature (*sva-bhAva*) and to the training that one gets due to the environment and upbringing. This is not denied by Hindu metaphysics. But the tendencies that one brings along from one's own past, including all previous lives, also contribute to the *sva- bhAva* or own-nature. The aggregate of behavior that results thus is broadly categorized into three major categories by Indian metaphysics. These are three categories of behavior, called *guNas*.

These are: *satva, rajas* and *tamas,* meaning roughly, divine, dynamic and dark (or dull). In reality no man or woman has any one of these in an exclusive manner. It is always a mixture of the three. These are the three strands which constitute the *prakRti*. *PrakRti* of course means Nature, in general, but actually stands for it in its broadest sense encompassing the entire universe of matter and material, in fact anything which is inert. They are actually Nature's concomitant and indispensable strands

- *satva is that of equilibrium and serenity.*
- *rajas is that of dynamism and kinesis.*
- *tamas is that of ignorance and inertia.*

They are inextricably interwoven in all forms of cosmic existence and phenomenon The imperishable resident of the body, namely the *jIva* or the individual soul, is by itself free but what binds it to the transmigratory cycle of births and deaths is the *prakRti* through the three *guNas*. Of these, the *rajo-guNa* is made up of desire, attraction, repulsion, likes and dislikes, and attachment to objects of desire. It binds man by repeatedly involving him in the dynamics of work. Dynamism broadly includes excitement, reaction to action, a constant distraction and so an antithesis to peace and calm. It attaches one to action. The *tamo-guNa* is born out of ignorance and deludes man from his real nature.

It binds man by the dark qualities of indolence, sleep and negligence. It attaches him to error and inaction. The *satva-guNa* because of its purity of quality is the cause of light and illumination. It binds man, however, by creating an attachment to knowledge, happiness and bliss.

As we observed earlier, it is the qualities inherent in the Cosmic Energy that gives matter its substance. Mind itself is matter. It is the effect of the play of Prakriti. The latter, individualised to each soul is the unmanifested factor, which, in consequence of the good and bad performances in the previous lives, has begun to give fruition in this life. This unmanifested factor is what is called *vAsanA,* but the Gita never uses the word *vAsanA*. It uses the word *avyakta,* which means, the unmanifested factor. This *avyakta* can be individual or collective. This totality of the unmanifested factor, in its macrocosmic aspect is the source of the whole universe at the beginning of creation. It is because of that the *Jiva* is under the spell of *mAyA* or *PrakRti* – through which Brahman functions to bring about the universe of men and things. The play of matter and Spirit in this manner is *samsAra*. The *Purusha* by himself has no *samsAra*. But when he identifies himself with the body, mind and senses which are the effects of *PrakRti*, he becomes the experiencer. Every action of the world as well as of the BMI is dominated by *PrakRti*. By coercing it and suppressing it violently you cannot win over it. This is the meaning of the famous verse III-33 of the Gita:

sadRRishaM ceshhTate svasyAH prakRRiter-jnAnavAnapi /

prakRRitiM yAnti bhUtAni nigrahaH kiM karishhyati //

Usually the common man and the unwise interpret this verse to mean that whatever we do is according to *PrakRti* and so there is nothing under our control. And one stretches the meaning to conclude that we are total slaves of our Fate – and this verse is very often cited to condemn Hinduism as a fatalist religion. The verse simply means: All beings, even the wise men, follow their own nature; what can coercion or restraint do? This means that coercion, or a suppression of, and violent resistance to, one's *svabhava* (= own nature and becoming) will be of no avail. But this is not a cry of despair. We do not have to resign ourselves to the wayward tendencies of our mind, inherited by its *vAsanAs*. The use of the word *'nigraha'* is significant. What is decried is *'nigrah'*, coercion, violent resistance and suppression. In the very next verse and in scores of other places Krishna extols *'samyama'* self-control, disciplined restraint, and practice in controlling the senses. We have to give due respect to the devil of our own *svabhava,* which is our own speciality of a *Prakriti,* go along with it and in due time control it, as much as possible. This shloka is an excellent example of how Hinduism, instead of being a fatalistic and pessimistic religion, is actually very realistic and constructive.

Finally, Krishna uses the word *PrakRiti* at the most appropriate moment in his lecture to Arjuna. Almost at the end of his *Gitopadesha,* he finally gives this most important warning to Arjuna. In shloka 59 of chapter 18 he warns Arjuna as a final word: "If pushed by your ego, Arjuna, you decide not to fight this battle, your resolution is a waste because your *PraKRiti* will control you and you will be made to fight.

CHAPTER 9

I

The 'I' is nearer to us than our eyes and ears. It is the soul of our souls. Whether it is childhood or adulthood we refer to ourselves by the same 'I'. It is not the body nor the senses nor the intellect nor the vital air of breath which sustains our life, nor any combination or conglomeration of these. It is nothing that is included in all that we call 'mine'. Write out all that goes under the list of what we might want to call 'mine'. This must include not only one's physical possessions, but also one's own body and its limbs, mind, mental opinions, anything which can go under 'my ....'. Throw out ALL THIS and then what remains is 'I'. This I is the Self of the Upanishads. This Self, they say, is just the Brahman that transcends everything. The Self is known by the word 'Atman'.

Anything that we call 'this' or 'ours' is impermanent. Only the 'I' embedded in our self is permanent. For this 'I' never changes, inspite of our aging, inspite of the passage of time and inspite of a change in location. So neither time nor space causes a change to this 'I', though, of course, anything 'connected' with this 'I' does get affected by time, space and causation. The

Upanishadic seers have done a substantial research on this question. Who is this 'I' that seems to be never-changing? In this connection they analyse the daily event of sleep. We say 'I slept well'. Who slept well? Who remembers the pleasure of sleeping? Certainly it is not the mind because it was itself sleeping. If it were not sleeping it would have been dreaming. Then who has enjoyed the pleasure of sleeping and now remembers it? *The scriptures say that it is the 'I' which is a permanent witness to all the happenings, and which is the substratum of all that can be called mine.*

That witness is the Atman which is spoken of in the scriptures as

SOUNDLESS, FORMLESS, INTANGIBLE, UNDYING, TASTELESS, ODOURLESS, WITHOUT BEGINNING, WITHOUT END, ETERNAL, IMMUTABLE AND BEYOND NATURE.

> *"ashabdam, asparsham, arUpam, avyayam, tathA arasam, nityam, agandhavaccha yat; anAdyanantam mahataH param dhruvam ..."*

(Katha Upanishad: 1-3-15)

Its own nature is perfect bliss and perfect knowledge.

A true renouncer knows that the only way to live in the world and not be attached to it is to attach oneself to God. That this is the same thing as attaching oneself to the Atman is the advaitic conclusion. The 'I' of such a devotee does him or anybody no harm. It is like a 'sword, which after touching the philosopher's stone, turns into gold; and therefore, cuts no more and injures none' (Quotation from Sri Ramakrishna). Only the form or the mark of the ego is left in such a person like the dry leaves of a coconut tree that have dropped off in the wind leaving marks on the trunk; those marks only show they were leaves at one time.

Renunciation of doership is the negation of the false idea of ourselves as the doer. The body does not claim any proprietorship for the 'I'-feeling. The Atman does no function, so it does not claim the 'I'-feeling. In between, the feeling of 'I' is born in the whole system consisting of the body and mind. It is actually a knot (called *'granthi'* in Tamil works of Ramana Maharishi) between Consciousness and the Inert *(jaDam)*. This knot is 'the bondage, the individual soul, the subtle body, egoism, *samsAra* and the mind'. (Quotation from Ramana). Cutting the knot is *sannyAsa,* physical renunciation; loosening the knot and making it ripe for cutting is *tyAga,* inner renunciation. <u>The latter should always precede the former.</u>

The advaita school holds that the individual self minus its ego as well as its *avidyA* (= Ignorance arising from its *vAsanAs*) is nothing but the Absolute Self. So when the individual self is said to surrender to the higher Self, what is surrendered and sacrificed to the Subject is the ego. The thought of proprietorship of action, namely that 'I am the doer (*KartA*)', 'I am the experiencer (*BhoktA*)' – this *parigraha,* i.e., mental possession of possessorship and doership, is what is renounced and surrendered.

By the oft-quoted statement 'Renouncing all dharmas' (*sarva-dharmAn parityajya* – Gita 18-66) what is sought to be renounced is the dharma of being the possessor and doer of all actions, words and thoughts. 'I' and 'Mine' are the two great evils in the mind. Instead of identifying ourselves with the real 'I' who is deep within us as the Subject, we always confuse 'I' with the body, mind and its ramifications. This is '*dehAtma-buddhi*'. It is the feeling that this Self is the conglomeration of several things external to it like the body, etc. It is this false dharma that has to be renounced. Once it is done then what remains is the Subject and Subject alone. There is no second. The surrender is complete.

This is the apex of both Bhakti and *jnAna*. Our true nature is Divinity and becoming divine is most natural to us. In that natural state one loves all human beings and the love to the Personal Manifestation of the Impersonal is a spontaneous effervescence. This is *parA* bhakti – Devotion par excellence. It knows no 'I' or 'Mine'. The little self is merged in the Supreme Self. Knowledge and Ignorance both get consumed in that oneness of the knower, the known and knowledge. There is no seer, no vision, nothing to be seen.

For such a brahma-*jnAni*, neither time nor action, neither merit nor demerit, neither pleasure nor pain, matters the least. In that state of Enlightenment, there is no distinction between oneself and the other self. It is full of Grace and Light – no darkness, no confusion. It is the massive Light of Consciousness. No up, no down; no high, no low; no peak, no valley. It is a state that transcends speech and mind, a state that has no goings-on, no action, no reaction. Who can describe such a state? Only a confirmed brahma-*jnAni* like Adi Shankara can vocalise it into poetry thus:

'No merit, no demerit, no happiness, no misery, no chants, no holy water, no scriptures, no rituals. I am neither the experiencer, nor the experienced, not also the experience. I am Consciousness, I am Bliss, I am Shiva'

na puNyam na pApam na soukhyam na dukham

na mantro na tIrtham na vedAH na yajnAH; aham bhojanam naiva bhojyam na bhoktA cidAnanda-rUpaH Shivo'ham Shivo'ham.

CHAPTER 10

Difference and Non- Difference

While the three major schools of philosophy in Hindu tradition agree that the Absolute Transcendental Supreme is ever-present, all-knowing and all-powerful, in relation to God or the Ultimate, the nature of the Soul (or the *Jiva*) and the Universe is differently interpreted by the three schools.

The *advaita* school says there is only one Absolute Reality. *Jiva* and Universe are ultimately the same as the essential Divinity, that is called brahman in the Upanishads. It is infinite in its presence, infinite in its consciousness and infinite in bliss. The Universe is only an appearance, superimposed on the Transcendent Reality. The *Jiva* has an individual existence only so long as it is wrapped up in ignorance of its identity and therefore, a total merging of the *Jiva* with brahman. What appears as the external Universe is only a phenomenon born out of ignorance, a beginningless ignorance which ends when the release (= *moksha*) takes place. The plurality that we perceive during our period of Ignorance is only an apparent plurality. If that is taken as real then it is impossible to reconcile the experience of the sages with such a creed; because in that case Deliverance from *samsAra* (= the cycle of births and deaths) would have a beginning and then there is the inevitable consequence that such a deliverance must also have an end!

NOTE: Other than the *advaita* writers in English, the other schools do not make any specific distinction betwen *JIva* and the soul and they write as if both mean the same thing. We shall also follow them when we write about them

The *viSishTAdvaita* school led by Ramanuja says the Soul and Universe are only parts of the Absolute God. The relationship of God to the Soul and the Universe is like the relationship of the Soul of man to the body of man. Individual souls are therefore only parts of brahman. God, Soul and Universe together form an inseparable unity which is one and has no second. Matter and Souls inhere in that Ultimate Reality as attributes to a substance. *Cit (souls)* and *acit (matter)* are only the body of God. So though there is difference from God, this difference is subordinate to the non-difference. Creation is a real act of God. It is the expansion of intelligence. Matter is fundamentally real and undergoes real revelation. The Soul is a higher mode than matter, because it is conscious. It is also eternally real and eternally distinct. Final release is a communion with God. Individual Souls retain their separate identities even after *moksha.* They live in fellowship with God either serving Him or meditating on Him.

The *dvaita* school led by *Madhwa* says that God, Soul and Universe are three mutually and fundamentally different categories, each having a separate reality, though the latter two are dependent on the former. However, God controls them. God's Grace is necessary for the liberation of the Soul. God is only the Agent. He causes the universe to be born and controls it. But He is not its material cause. Five differences are absolute: God and Soul; Soul and Soul; God and Matter; Soul and Matter; Matter and Matter. Each Soul is essentially different and belongs to different grace, even in its enjoyment of bliss after moksha. The philosophy is one of down-to-earth realism. *Vyasaraja,* one of the triumvirate-giants of this school – the other two being *Madhwa* and *Jayatirtha* - summarises the entire philosophy in a set of nine points:

- Lord Narayana is possessed of countless qualities, is devoid of all blemish and is an independent Reality.
- He creates and sustains the world.
- He is the One who grants moksha to pious souls;
- The universe is real.
- There is a five-fold difference.
- Souls are dependent on God.
- All souls are not alike.

- Moksha is a state of existence when the soul enjoyseternal bliss; the only way to reach that state is Devotion.
- The Lord can be only known through Scriptures.

Delving deep into the three schools academically, one finds that the distinguishing characteristics of the three schools may be classified in terms of the three fundamental concepts of the idea of Difference (= *bheda*):

sajAtIya-bheda: Difference within the same category

Within the category of trees there are, for example, apple trees and lemon trees.

This difference that exists among trees in the category of all trees is *sajAtIya-bheda.*

Such a difference does not exist in the category of brahman, the Absolute Reality.

In other words, brahman is unique in its category. There is no second brahman.

On this point the three major schools of *vedanta* agree.

All of them say brahman is unique in itself. In brahman, there is no *sajAtIya-bheda.*

vijAtIya-bheda: Inter-category Difference

There is the category of trees and there is the category of hills.

Trees and hills belong to different categories.

Such an inter-category difference does not exist with respect to brahman, say both Sankara and Ramanuja. There is only one category, brahman and everything is brahman, says Sankara.

And Ramanuja says: there is only one category, brahman and everything else is a part of it.

But *Madhwa* maintains that the category of individual souls and the category of universe are categories different from brahman and so, even from the absolute point of view there is inter-category difference; and, further, this distinction between categories is absolute and unqualified.

For *Madhwa's* school the souls and the universe are essentially different and distinct from brahman.

svagata-bheda: Difference of the entity within itself

Within a tree, there are branches, leaves, flowers, fruits, etc.

These are by themselves different from the tree though together they all make the tree.

The tree is therefore said to have *svagata-bheda.*

According to Sankara, brahman does not have even this difference within itself. It is whole, without parts, bereft of attributes and distinctions. This is Sankara's reading of the Upanishads.

Ramanuja as well as Madhwa differ from this.

All the three agree that brahman is Existence-Knowledge-Bliss.

But Sankara says these three refer to one and the same undiversified attributeless brahman, because they are identical in essence and each one of them is a definition and not a qualification of brahman.

The other two schools opine these are the three essential features of brahman who is therefore possessed of attributes and distinctions.

To sum up, we may state the same in terms of a concept of non-difference. As far as God, Souls and Universe are concerned, Sankara says there is non-difference of all the three varieties. Ramanuja and *Madhwa* both agree with Sankara on the *sajAtIya* non-difference, meaning thereby that there is no such thing as a second brahman. However *Madhwa* asserts that the other two kinds of difference persist. However, between Sankara and Ramanuja there is agreement on two types of non- difference. Their only difference is on the *svagata- bheda*. Within God there is a soul-body relationship between God and the Universe of Matter and Souls and therefore there is *svagata-bheda* in brahman according to Ramanuja. But Sankara and Ramanuja both agree that Matter emanated from brahman as is declared in statements like

'That itself manifested itself'

(= *tad AtmAnaM svayaM akuruta*)

– taittirIya upanishad II - 7

The universe is only a modification of brahman, in both the *advaita* and *viSisTAdvaita* philosophies; but hold on, there is a crucial difference between the two viewpoints.

The *advaita* view says that the modification is only apparent, while the *viSishTAdvaita* view says that the modification is real!

To use another metaphor from the modern world of technology,

advaita says that the modified appearance of brahman as the universe is a projection like a movie and therefore comparatively unreal,

while the *viSishTadvaita* view says that the modification is an actual play on the stage and therefore real!

What matters is not how the three Masters differ on the facets of difference and non-difference among the three entities: God, Souls and Universe; what matters is the non-difference in their teaching to humanity in regard to what one has to do in the daily world. It is interesting to note at this point that to whatever school a noted saint or devotee belongs his prayers or compositions always include the thought that whatever birth he may have to take in the future, whatever number of times he may have to be born in the future, his only prayer is that he should not forget the name of God. *The unity of Indian culture should be seen in such common characteristic prayers.* Every saint would say that our needs and desires are endless and so in our prayers to God we must not seek anything except devotion to Him. *In fact this is why Hindu religion is one in spite of all the differences in the interpretations of scriptures.* Any attempt to sort out these differences at an intellectual level may become just an exercise in futility. Well might one echo with Jagadguru Sankaracharya of Sringeri:

> **'You cannot see the feet of the Lord, why do you waste time debating about the nature of His face?'**

The very nature of the literature of the Upanishads does not allow one unique interpretation. The Upanishads, as we know, are collections of free candid and detailed discussions between teacher and disciple and it is for the reader to draw his or her own conclusion after assimilating the analysis thus presented and in the light of one's own spiritual experience. It is here that the great *AcAryas* help. Even to understand them one will need the physical presence of a *guru*. It is therefore not fair to expect the Upanishads to tell us whether this is right or that is wrong. To follow one of these masters with single-minded faith and try to understand that master and his perception of what the Upanishads say might itself occupy a whole life-time.

For the ordinary busy intelligent layman of the modern world, it will become a crisis of intellect to ask questions like:

Is the advaita of Sankara the correct interpretation of the Upanishads or not? Is not the *viSishTAdvaita* explanation of Ramanuja the ultimate answer?

Which of the three great Masters has the correct philosophy applicable to our daily life? To which of the statements in the Upanishads shall we give importance or dominance? -

To the statements that are obviously absolutist, as recommended by Sankara? Or to those that are obviously non-absolutist as recommended by Madhwa and Ramanuja?

Such differences in interpretation has generated a succession of philosophical literature by later thinkers and writers and the body of literature on both sides is nothing but voluminous. Instead of trying to arbitrate among the great Masters, we should only aim to understand one of them in as much fullness as possible. This one Master may be chosen, as per one's tradition, taste, attitudes and upbringing. In saying this we certainly invite the criticism that Hinduism is too tolerant. But, is there something like too rich a man or too beautiful a woman?

CHAPTER 11

Adi Shankara's Message of Oneness

'The scriptures are innumerable; the things to be known are many; the time at our disposal is short; the obstacles are too many. It is therefore important to grasp the essence and essence only'

ananta-shAstraM bahu veditavyaM alpaSca kAlo bahavaSca vighnAH / yat-sAra-bhUtam tad-upAsitavyaM

hamso yathA kshIram-ivAmbhu-rASau //

It is in this sense that we should approach the message of one-ness taught by the Advaita school led by Shankara. The philosophy that Shankara propagated was not his own. It was already in the Upanishads. What he did was to focus his searchlight on it and prove to us that it was the central and only teaching of the Upanishads as well as their collective last word. But the ordinary layman who remembers Shankara now does not know enough about him or his philosophy to understand him well. The only thing he can say is that Shankara taught about *mAyA* or illusion. 'Illusion' is a wrong translation of *mAyA*. By translating *mAyA* as illusion we have done the greatest disservice to Shankara. <u>It is not being said that the world does not exist. It is only being said that the world is an appearance, not totally real.</u> Shankara distinguishes three orders of reality.

- The Absolute Reality, that is Brahman and Brahman alone.
- The complete unreality, like the horns of a hare, or like squaring the circle if one wants to use the modern scientific language.
- In between these two extremes there is a phenomenal (or subjective) reality which is the apparent reality of the dream world, and an empirical (or operational) reality which is the 'reality' of the world of experience by the senses. Both these realities are classified as *MithyA* in *advaita vedanta*, because the reality is not absolute. *MithyA* is a technical word in *advaita*, not to be understood as 'illusion'. <u>*It is that which is neither unreal (because it appears) nor real (since later it disappears). Therefore it is anirvacanIyA, 'indescribable'.*</u>

G.S. Murty *(Para-tattva-ganita-darSanam, 2002))* writes: *MithyA* is Empirical Truth or a corrupted form of Truth. The meaning can be illustrated by an example from television. If the original image is distorted due to an error in transmission, the distorted image is the empirical truth. It is false only by comparison with the original.

A dream is neither real nor unreal. It is real to the person who dreams. It is unreal to the same person after he wakes up from the dream. This is the most important point. A dream is not a dream or illusion to the dreamer. So long as we dream, so long as we are seeing only the plurality of this mundane world, it is as real to us as the dream is to the dreamer. The world is unreal only to the seer who has woken up to the reality of the Absolute – like a Ramana *MahaRshi* or a SadaShiva Brahmendra. For them the only real thing is the Absolute Brahman. What they see before them is also Brahman. They see Brahman everywhere. So the world has not vanished absolutely. The world has vanished from their point of view. So if they keep on telling you that the world is an illusion or *mithyA*, it is like someone appearing in your dream and telling you, you better wake up from the dream and wake up to the reality. We are so much engrossed in our dream that we are not prepared to listen to the advice of the guru or the Upanishads or to Shankara. Thus between the Ultimate Reality of the formless and nameless Absolute and the total unreality of non-existence, there is the intermediary apparent reality of this phenomenal world – which appears to be real but is not absolutely real. This appearance of the world as a reality has been given several analogies by philosophers. The most telling example of this is that of a rope appearing in twilight as a snake. The snake was never there. Even when the snake was being seen there was only the rope. The rope appeared as the snake. So also Brahman appears to us as the world. Even when the world is being seen it is Brahman that is being seen as the world. This the seers do know and so what they see is not the world but Brahman. One may object to this analogy as follows. I realise that there was no snake. So the snake no more appears to me. In the same manner I realise that there is only Brahman and there is no reality of the world. But still the world is appearing to me. For this Ramana *MahaRshi* asks you to go to the example of the mirage. The water in the mirage is only an illusion. I see the water in the mirage. I go near it and realise that there is no water. But once I come back I see there is again the appearance of the water. This analogy is to tell you that how even after realisation, the illusion may still appear as real.

Let us accept that any analogy has its own limitation. The analogies have to be taken only to that extent where we do not overdo it. Once the point of the analogy is made, there is no use in continuing the analogy. Thus here the objection is raised as follows. The water of the mirage does not quench my thirst, but in this supposedly unreal world, I have my thirst, hunger etc. and all these are quenched by the happenings in this world. For this Ramana asks you to look at the analogy of the dream. Within the dream you may have thirst, and it may be quenched by the water in the dream; so also hunger. Dream analogy is a great blessing. What else is a dream for? In God's creation, the value of a dream seems to be only this: To tell you how unreal is the world. Without the dream analogy it is impossible even to mentally conceive of the possible unreality of the phenomenal world from a different point of view, namely the absolute point of view. A dreamer wakes up usually only when something unpleasant happens within his dream. No dreamer ends up his dream while still in the happy state, except when an external force acts. This is because man's natural state is happiness. Realisation of one's natural state of happiness is *moksha,* according to Shankara. A complete absorption of the body-mind-intellect in this eternal state of knowledge and happiness is realisation of one's self. In order to do this one has not to chase it or do anything else, says Shankara. The removal of Ignorance is the only thing to be done. Automatically our natural state will be realised.

So what are we supposed to do at all? Shankara says: Do an introspection and investigate about your self starting the probing from a ruthless analysis of your own mind and its vagaries. Try to get away from its external occupations and make it preoccupied with questions like; What is making the mind think? What is really behind it? Who is the thinker? Why are you not able to control the mind? What is more permanent than the mind? Wherefrom does the mind derive its strength? Besides the physical brain where the external hardware processes the thoughts of the mind, what is the software that forms the source for all the vibrations of the mind? Whence does it spring forth? Who is operating this software? If the answer comes up saying that it is you who are operating the software, then is that 'you' different from the 'you' which stands behind, watching the mind? Can you watch the mind unperturbed by any of its goings-on? In that sense can you still the mind? Now who is this 'you'? Shankara and all the other exponents of advaita plead with us to keep on asking these questions and try to get convincing answers within *oneself* from oneself. Certainly they also ask us to go to a teacher and go through the *shravaNa* discipline.. But a teacher can only point the way. The final analysis has to be done by oneself on and for oneself by *manana* and *nididhyAsana* (introspective contemplation). Seers have declared emphatically that the quality and intensity of the internal struggle to get at these answers differ from person to person and it depends upon one's stage of spiritual evolution and the struggle he has already put in through all his various lives.

The person who is already spiritually ripe because of his earlier *vAsanA,* will probably get the enlightenment just by one listening to the teaching from the guru. But for the rest of us who are still far below this stage, Shankara says: 'Occupy your mind with God rather than with such secular pursuits as learning the gymnastics of rules of grammar'.

bhaja GovindaM bhaja GovindaM GovindaM bhaja mUDhamate;

saMprApte sannihite kAle na hi na hi rakshati dukRngkaraNe.

'Seek the company of the good. Through the company of the good *(sat-sangam)* there arises non-attachment; through non-attachment, there arises freedom from delusion; through delusionlessness, there arises steadfastness; through steadfastness, there arises liberation in life.'

satsangatve nissangatvaM nissangatve

nirmohatvaM; nirmohatve

niSchalatatvaM niSchalatatve

JIvanmuktiH

In this context, it is important to note that, throughout the length and breadth of India, and through all the centuries, the concept of *sat-sangh* has been emphasized in every scripture and almost every literary work, that one cannot miss to note it as the sine-qua-non for spiritual uplift. Listen to the noblest of the noble souls, Tulsi from his *Ram-charita- mAnas*: 'Of the various creatures, both animate and inanimate, living in this world, whether in water or on land or in the air, whoever has ever attained wisdom, glory, salvation, material prosperity or welfare anywhere and by any means whatsoever, know it to be the result of association with holy men; there is no other means either in this world or in the Vedas'.

Do not be proud of wealth, kith and kin, and youth; Time takes away all these in a jiffy. Leaving aside this entire world which is transitory, and knowing the state of Brahman, enter into it –

mA kuru dhana-jana-yauvana-garvaM

harati nimeshhAt-kAlas-sarvaM; mAyA-mayam-idam-akhilaM hitvA

Brahma-padaM tvam pravisha viditvA

continues Shankara in his Bhaja-Govindam. Sing the song of the Gita. Recite and revel in the one thousand names of Vishnu. Meditate on the form of the Goddess. Take the mind into the company of the good. Distribute wealth among the needy. Be devoted completely to the lotus-feet of the Master. Then, through the discipline of the mind and the control of the senses you can behold the Absolute who resides in your heart. Make no difference between the God Absolute and the Master to whom you have surrendered. Even matters that have not been explicitly declared in the scriptures will become manifest to such a seeker. It is interesting to note that this meaning comes out from a famous verse in Svetashvatara Upanishad.6-23: Whoever has superlative bhakti in God and as to God so to the Guru, to that great soul will the meanings spoken of here will sprout

Yasya deve parA bhaktiH yathA deve tathA gurau /

tasyaite kathitAhyarthAH prakASante mahAtmanaH

But great exponents split the words '*tasyaite kathitAhyarthAH*' as '*tasyaite + akathitAhyarthAH*' (the grammar allows this!) and now it means: …even unspelt meanings sprout in him!

So it all comes down to Devotion to the Absolute, or devotion to the guru who is nothing but the Absolute. In such a devotion, there is to be no distinction between God and God. The usual talk among the masses about the worship of Shiva or Vishnu (the two major Gods of the Hindu trinity) being two contrary disciplines does not make sense to Shankara. There is not only no difference; they are one and the same. The Absolute in two garbs, that is all. Shankara is so convinced about the importance of this non-difference that he prays to God in his Gangashtakam, verse #8,, as if he were afraid that he himself might get lost and lose his conviction in this maze of confusion prevalent in this world

mātarjāhnavī śambhusaṅgavalite maulai
nidhāyāñjalim

tvattīre vapuSo'vasānasamaye
nārāyaṇānghridvayam

sānandam smarato bhavishhyati mama
prāṇaprayāṇotsave

bhūyāt bhaktiravicyutā hariharadvaitātmikā
shAshvatI...

Hey mother Jahnavi, at the end of my wanderings devoted for search for the company of lord Shiva, the end celebration of my travel of the soul, Would happen in your bank, while I would be meditating, Holding my two hands in salute over my head, With happiness, on the lotus feet of Lord Vishnu. Let my devotion to Vishnu and Shiva be permanent, Oh Goddess.

The first step in understanding the non-dual philosophy of Shankara is this non-difference of Shiva and Vishnu. The next step is to realise that this one God is not only transcendent but also immanent in every one of the living beings. This makes Shankara define bhakti as nothing but the contemplation of one's real self. *(Viveka-chUDAmaNi #32: svasvarUpAnusandhAnaM bhaktir-ity- abhidhIyate)*. As oil dwells in the oil-seed, as curd in milk, as water in a ground-water source or as fire in firewood so does He dwell in the Universe – says Svetashvatara Upanishad. 1-15

tileshu tailam dadhinIshhu
sarpiH Apas
shrotashvaraNishhu
cAgniH.

This Absolute is everywhere, in front of us, behind us, above us, below us, to the right of us, to the left of us

– the scriptures do not tire of repeating this kind of refrain. And all this is in oneself, i.e. one's Self. This Self is everywhere. That is why the Ishavasya U. says: It is already there before even the fastest mind goes there. In the entire philosophical thought process of the world this thought that the whole universe is immanent in oneself is a giant leap for mankind. When the universe dissolves in the Ultimate, it is a stepwise dissolution. From earth to water, from water to fire, from fire to air, from air to space – these are the stages of dissolution. Finally what remains is Space. Even that space finally will dissolve in the Atman, says the scripture. Can we imagine this situation when there is nothing, not even space? It is to help us attempt the mental gymnastics of comprehending this that all the scriptures cry hoarse on this topic.

Great devotees and exponents of the Advaitic school (of Shankara) have extolled the qualities and pleasures of bhakti so eloquently that for the ordinary man there should be no doubt about the fundamental role of bhakti in advaita. But critics of advaita as well as laymen who have not cared to take the effort to understand what advaita is, do sometimes declare that bhakti is not concordant with the concept of advaita and to be a devotee is not the forte of an Advaitin. Their question is: how can bhakti coexist with advaita? According to them, the teaching (of advaita) that the Self of each individual is the same as the Supreme Self is contradictory to the duality implied in the concept of bhakti. In the process of devotion there is always a duality involved - namely, the worshipper and the worshipped. If God or the Supreme Reality does not have a separate status other than our Selves, then who is to worship whom? advaita means non- duality. There is no second object in existence other than the Supreme

Godhead. So where is the leeway for any worship or devotion? Recall his Shivanandalahari Verse No.81. It is the same Shankara who declares through all his commentaries and prakarana-granthas that Knowledge alone – neither an integration of Knowledge and Works nor an integration of Knowledge and Devotion – that leads to moksha. But to get to that state of Knowledge where one perceives nothing else, because there is only the Perceiver, he strongly recommends the doing of Works in a desireless unattached way and with a one-pointed devotion to the Ultimate. In order to impress upon us laymen that this is the only way to ascend to spiritual heights, he tours the whole country more than once, visits almost every important temple and place of pilgrimage and sings his compositions in praise of the revered deities of that place in the most eloquent poetry. He it is who has established the tradition of ritually worshipping together all the five divinities – *sUrya*, the Sun-God; Shakti, the Mother; Vishnu, *gaNeSa* and Shiva – of the Hindu tradition through the *pancAyatanapUjA* way. It is because of this worship of the formless as if it has a form, that invocation mantras in the advaitic tradition contain effectively the following idea as the core of the mantra. 'Oh God! I know you are omnipresent. But, for the purpose of my concentration and worship please condescend to make your presence felt here in this idol (image, picture or stone or whatever) for the period of the *pUjA*; maybe I am insulting your omnipresence by requesting you to confine yourself to this form and space, but please pardon me; I know no other way'.

The ascent from our physical, vital, emotional and intellectual being into the supermind of spiritual being is spiritual evolution. The technology of this ascent is Spiritual Love. There are at least three stages through which one has to rise. The first is *bAhya* bhakti or external bhakti. This is adoration of something outside ourselves. It is based on the unenlightened *tAmasik* feeling that God is external to us and that He dwells in a particular locality – a temple, a shrine or a holy place or bathing *ghAT*. Popular religion does not usually rise above this level. The second stage of bhakti is *ananya* bhakti, the exclusive and passionate *(rAjasik)* worship of one's favourite deity. It is in fact an intense monotheism. The entire Ram-carita-manas of Tulsidas is a monumental example of the purity and majesty of *ananya*-bhakti. The third stage of bhakti is *ekAnta* bhakti, the purest *(sAtvik)* form. Here the worshipper loves God for His own sake and not for His gifts, not even for moksha. It is free from the feeling for any other object. It is the service of the Lord – an adoring service that implies centering of the mind on Him, expecting no gain either here or hereafter. It is a constant flow of mind, brimming with love towards the Lord and His creation, without any selfish desire. All his activities are sublimated into worship of the Divine. Whatever he does, whatever he eats, whatever he offers, is all a dedication to the Divine, not just as a formality, as ordinary virtuous people profess to be doing, but in total reality (B.G. 9-27). Such a devotee appears to be doing external activities but since his ego is in total sublimation to the Divine he is not doing anything for himself. Even the distinction between sacred and secular activity disappears in such a soul. Every work is sacred to him inasmuch as it is an expression of his love of God. This supreme love of God was expressed by the cowherdesses of Brindavan. Their love can be understood by us only if, in the words of Swami VivekAnanda 'we can forget our love of gold, name and fame and this little material world of ours'. Their love, even though it originated in a kind of physical desire, rose up to the highest plane of self-effacing love of God, because of the holy association of the Divine, and thus in its final stages became the pinnacle of perfection of bhakti. The artistic manifestation of this bhakti can take place in one or more of nine ways – says Prahlad, the Devotee par excellence. This statement of his occurs as a spirited reply of a boy of five years old to the arrogant father's seemingly innocent query about the former's progress in his study-in-residence with the guru. It is one of the grandest pronouncements of the Hindu religion, that has since been quoted across the world millions of times.

It is not the name of the deity, Vishnu or Narayana, that is important here. The name is not there to distinguish it from the other names of God. This is the purport of advaita. Whether it is Shiva or Vishnu, all the references are only to the One Supreme God – this is the intent of the Vedas.

'They are the same; just as the same actor appears in different roles, one is the Paramatma (Transcendental Supreme) dressed as Vishnu and the other is Paramatma dressed as Shiva, says the Mahaswami of Kanchi. Throughout the vedic literature one will find various divinities Varuna, Indra, Soma, Agni and Surya each glorified at one point to the exclusion of everything else. Any attempt to dissect the meanings and find a logical hierarchical explanation in the worldly literary sense of characters in literary fiction, would fail miserably. The entire mythological set-up embedded in the multitude of our *PurANas*, if taken at their story-value without any feeling for the under- current of the oneness of the Almighty, will create nothing but chaos in our intellectual understanding. The different hymns eulogising the different gods and goddesses are couched either in simple language with complex meanings or in complex language which perhaps hide simple ideas. It is very easy to misunderstand their significance and meanings. Western interpreters who have not got into the spirit of the religion have erred in a colossal manner. If you carefully look at the superlatives being used in the Vedic literature in the same manner and language for each Vedic deity and if you look at the exact imitations of these eulogies made by the PurANas for the various other manifestations of the Ultimate Divinity, one cannot but conclude that the last words of the Vedas are those passages where each such deity is considered as only one expression of the same many-faceted supreme Almighty. One such passage from the Aitareya Upanishad (III-1-1) raises the question: Who is this Self, whom we desire to worship? Is he the self by which we see, hear, etc.? Is he the heart and mind by which we perceive? No, says the Upanishad (III-1-3). These are but adjuncts of the Self. The Self itself is Pure Consciousness. He is Brahman. He is God, He is BrahmA, He is Indra, He is all Gods; the five elements – earth air space, water fire; all beings, great or small, born of eggs, born from the womb, born from heat, born from soil; horses, cows, men, elephants, birds; everything that breathes, the beings that walk and the beings that walk not, the beings that fly and those that fly not. The reality behind all these is Brahman, who is pure Consciousness. Consciousness is Brahman. *prajnAnaM Brahma.*

The natural state of each individual is the state of being Brahman, say the scriptures. Shankara therefore defines bhakti in specific terms as contemplative living in one's natural state, that is, the divine state. This *brahma-bhAva,* being in Brahman, automatically implies an equanimous view of every being in the world as the same self as the one dwells in the seer. This balanced view of everything as One, everything as the Self, is a blissful experience, called brahma- Ananda. It does not come out of studies or scholarship. It is a state to be enjoyed internally, not by the external apparatus. When that experience crystallises, there is no more knowledge, no more ignorance, no perceiver, nothing perceived, no perception. All that is seen by these enlightened souls is the godliness of Infinite Love and the loveliness of the Omnipresent God.

Shankara talks unceasingly about such a state of supreme bhakti, which we call advaita bhakti, in glowing terms. This poetic but precise description of Shankara is very often quoted as the thesis on bhakti. It is verse no.61 of ShivAnandalahari. It gives five analogies for bhakti or Devotion to Divinity. The first one cites what is called an ankola tree which has the characteristic that when its seeds fall from the tree on the ground and mature, they travel to the base of the tree and join the roots by their own nature. Just as these seeds reach the tree with a one-pointed purpose, so also the devotee should be devoted to his God of devotion – is the theme. The second analogy is that of iron filings that are drawn to a magnet. In these two analogies the duality of the components of the system involved is all but obvious. The next two analogies are that of a chaste wife being devoted and drawn towards her husband and that of a creeper which winds around a parent tree. In these two cases the quality of the relationship is certainly different from that of the first two analogies but still some duality remains. The fifth analogy is that of a river which is irrevocably bound to a path towards the ocean, its ultimate destination. It appears it is this analogy that is closest to the heart of Adi Shankara as far as his definition of bhakti is concerned.

Think of a golden ring. Does gold have the form of a ring? Goldness has nothing to do with the shape of a ring or roundness. The roundness of the ring is extraneous to gold. Do not see the ring, see only the gold, they say. This is why even words fail when the Vedas want to describe the Ultimate. 'What is not uttered by speech but that by which speech is revealed

is Brahman, not the thing that is before you', says

Kena Upanishad I-5.

> *yad vAcA anabhyuditam yena vAg-*
> *abhyudyate;*

> *tadeva brahmatvam viddhi nedaM*
> *yadidaM upAsate*

It is something which the words cannot describe, eyes cannot see, the ears cannot hear. Even the senses cannot sense it. How can the Seer see himself? How can the Knower know himself? So somehow out of all the multiplicity that is visible to us we have to see and sense the unity which is our own Self.

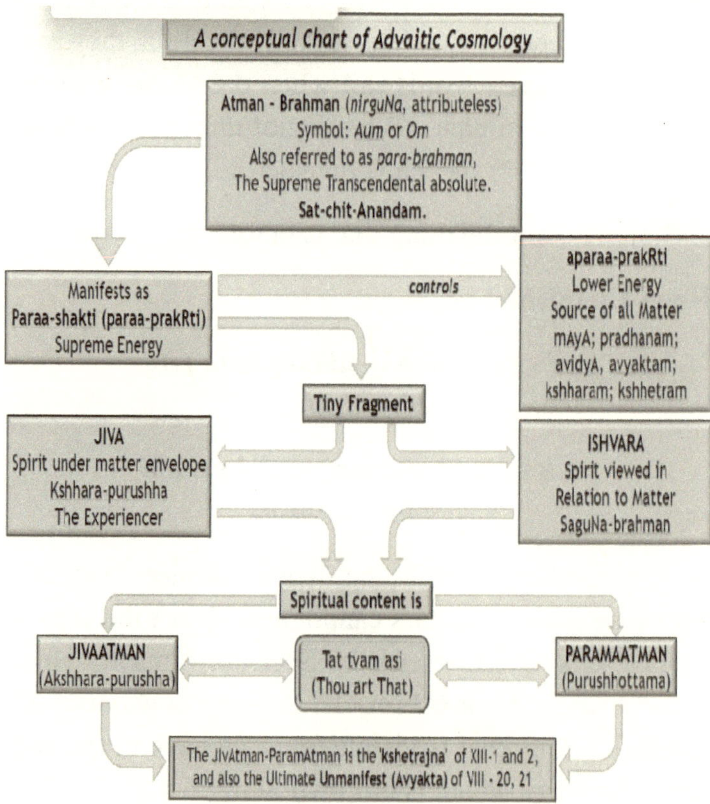
A conceptual Chart of Advaitic Cosmology

Atman - Brahman (nirguNa, attributeless)
Symbol: Aum or Om
Also referred to as para-brahman,
The Supreme Transcendental absolute.
Sat-chit-Anandam.

Manifests as
Paraa-shakti (paraa-prakRti)
Supreme Energy

controls

aparaa-prakRti
Lower Energy
Source of all Matter
mayA; pradhanam;
avidyA, avyaktam;
kshharam; kshhetram

Tiny Fragment

JIVA
Spirit under matter envelope
Kshhara-purushha
The Experiencer

ISHVARA
Spirit viewed in
Relation to Matter
SaguNa-brahman

Spiritual content is

JIVAATMAN
(Akshhara-purushha)

Tat tvam asi
(Thou art That)

PARAMAATMAN
(Purushhottama)

The JIvAtman-ParamAtman is the 'kshetrajna' of XIII-1 and 2,
and also the Ultimate Unmanifest (Avyakta) of VIII - 20, 21

CHAPTER 12

Non-Absolutist Schools

The seeds of the concept of bhakti go back to even the vedas. The plant of bhakti sprouts in the Upanishads; becomes a full-fledged plant in the *itihAsas,* particularly the *mahA-bhArata,* blossoms in the *PurANAs,* and flowers in the *Aagamas* both of the Saivite and *vaishNavite* varieties. The *AlvArs* and *nAyanmArs* bring out the fruits which ripen in the age of the *AcAryas* for all posterity to consume, enjoy and attain beatitude. The personal God with all His superlative attributes is worshipped mainly in six forms – *Shiva, Vishnu, Shakti, SUrya, GaNapati and SubrahmaNya.*

Among the various non-Absolutist conceptions of God Shri Ramanuja's is the most well known, has the largest following and has the claim to the longest tradition. It conceives of a Personal God with infinite divine attributes and infinite varieties of auspicious forms. He, however, is the single Conscious Entity that has all matter and all the JIvas as His body. He has infinite compassion for the JIvas and so He is greatly concerned about their salvation. The JIva has to comprehend this Inner Reality, rid itself of the three-fold miseries of life and merge in the infinite bliss of the eternal sanctity of God. This is *moksha.*

This is a communion with God, not a realization of complete identity. Those who desire this, should practise a seven-fold discipline – namely, the discretion of consuming only the right type of pure food; dispassion; the attitude of living in the presence of the Absolute; the action of the five daily rituals *(yajnas),* the ethics of a *dhArmic* life, absence of frustration and, finally, the absence of delusion caused by affluence and material happiness. Such a one does his duties as the dictates of the Lord and in total dedication to Him. This leads first to internal purity and in due time blesses one with the insight of Yoga wherein one can visualise the Spirit. That leads to the awareness of the JIva of all JIvas. Love of God pours forth spontaneously now. It is a self-forgetting Love that continues uninterruptedly like the pouring out of oil. This is the bhakti. The Lord may be conceived of as your guide, your master, your friend, your child, your beloved. Each one of these perfects the devotional attitude and ends up by creating the irresistible urge to see Him in person. That is the stage of bhakti par excellence. And when that vision of the Supreme Person sparks then is the stage of Supreme Enlightenment. Thereafter there is no return to the mundane living. The Lord then frees you from the bodily prison and takes you to His abode to live in fellowship with Him. The thing that makes this happen is only the Grace of the Lord and nothing else. That is why the Lord is said to be both the ultimate goal *(upeyaM)* as well as the path *(upAya)* to that goal. Such a faith ends up in the action of surrender to the Lord. Vedanta Desika lists eight kinds of devotion which epitomise the concept of spiritual love in a masterly fashion:

Feeling at home in the company of devotees; Enjoying the worship of the Lord; An unsatiated eagerness to listen to the stories of God; Horripilation and choking of voice when hearing about Him, talking to Him and remembering Him; Performing of ritual pujA to the deities; Not showing off one's service to God; Meditation of Him and Him only; and Praying to Him, never for mundane trivialities.

Nimbarka of the twelfth century propagated what is called *dvaitAdvaita* school of thinking; *dvaita* is duality and *advaita* is non-duality. According to Nimbarka the JIvas and the universe are different from the Absolute which rules them. Yet just as the spider's web though different from the spider which has woven it is still one with the spider because it is nothing but the saliva of the spider it is the Lord that has become the JIvas and the universe. Thus difference and non-difference are emphasized equally. Difference is when existence is separate though not independent. Non-difference is the impossibility of separate existence. Like the ocean and the waves, like the Sun and its Light, there is difference and at the same time non-difference. One should take the Absolute Brahman as the JIva of all JIvas and of the Universe, comprehend this difference-in-non-difference and surrender oneself to the Lord in toto. The attitude of Radha to Krishna is what is recommended by this school. Shrimad BhAgavatham. is the most respected scripture.

To the great *Madhwa-AcArya* (13th century) is to be attributed the credit for the massive propagation of the school of duality (dvaita). Lord Vishnu with all his attributes and forms is the Absolute Truth and God Almighty. The Lord is the infinite home of all auspicious qualities and has no material or detestable traits. His purpose of creation is to enable the individual JIva to work out his salvation through devotion and discipline. He has a tremendous compassion towards his creation. He gives men what they deserve according to their past karma and their present tendencies. He is the protector of every JIva. The three concepts *cit, acit and ISvara* are all three different. Lord Vishnu creates by his Will. Those who desire moksha should start from the hypothesis of God being the master and man his servant and live his life by serving Him and dwelling on the glories of God. This would generate the right bhakti in him. By doing God's will, one nurtures this bhakti. Finally by His Grace one attains salvation and experiences the state of Bliss in proportion to the *sAtvic* deeds he has done. The goal of life is to serve God both in this life and in the after-life. Bhakti is uninterrupted attachment to the Lord with complete understanding of His greatness transcending the love of one's own Self and possessions and which remain unshaken in the face of difficulties. The role model of this bhakti is Hanuman of the Ramayana. The entire philosophy of bhakti of this school is enjoyably summarised in a mini-encyclopaedic work - *hari-kathA-mRta-sAram* - of Jagannatha-dasa of the eighteenth century. That the Lord is such a compassionate One who takes ten steps towards you the moment you take one step towards Him is an accepted maxim of all schools of philosophy. But the dramatic and figurative way in which Jagannatha-dasa expresses this is inimitable. Says he: 'The Lord is always one step ahead. If the devotee prays from a reclining position, God sits and listens. If the devotee appeals sitting, God stands attentively. If the former stands, God walks around him and registers his requests. If he walks and prays, God displays his love by ecstatic dancing and jumping'! The conclusion of course is implied: If the devotee dances and jumps in his chanting, what will not He do for him?

VallabhAcArya of the 15th and 16th centuries spread the theory of *SuddhAdvaita*. According to this the glorious Krishna in His *sat-chid-Ananda* form is the Absolute Brahman. He is permanently playing out His sport (leela) from His seat in the goloka which is even beyond the divine *vaikunTHa,* the abode of Vishnu. Creation is His sport. To obtain the Bliss given out by Krishna the only path is bhakti. But in this age of kali, the scripture-sanctioned bhakti is impossible to practise. So what is recommended is *pushTi bhakti* – which we can all get from the natural Grace of God just like that, for no reason whatsoever. It is that bhakti which gives itself up body, heart and JIva to the cause of God. It is considered to be the fullest expression of what is known as *Atma-nivedana* (= giving-up of oneself) among the nine forms of bhakti. It is the bhakti of the devotee who worships God not for any reward or presents but for His own sake. Such a devotee goes to goloka after leaving this body and lives in eternal bliss enjoying the sports of the Lord. The classical example of this complete self- effacement is that of the cow-herdesses towards Krishna. They spoke no word except prayer and they moved no step except towards Krishna. Their supreme-most meditation was on the lotus-feet of Krishna.

Shri Krishna Chaitanya of the 16th century is universally known for his propagation, by excellent example of his own life, of the *acintya-bheda-abheda* philosophy and the conviction about the Radha- Krishna theme that popularised Radha as a Goddess and an Avatara of Lakshmi. The relationship between the Lord and His consort is that of difference within non-difference and is therefore mentally unimaginable. The Lord is having an eternal sport with Radha. By his charming sports and beautiful form He mesmerises Man, corrects him and blesses him. Bhakti is the only means to reach Him. By constant practice of the instruments of bhakti, and by cultivating a taste for the names of the Lord, compassion for the living, service to the servants of God, one increases one's component of *satva-guNa*

(=divine tendency) and his devotion now becomes a passion for the divine in due course. This leads step by step to a state of supreme ecstasy. To reach this one may start from the silent bhakti of Bhishma, move on to the *vAtsalya* (filial affection) bhakti of Yasoda, the friendly bhakti of Arjuna, the *dAsya bhakti* (devotion by a servant) of Hanuman and finally reaches the *mAdhura bhakti* (devotion of Love) of the gopis – where the relationship between the devotee and the Lord is that of the spouse to the beloved. This form of bhakti is most graphically portrayed in *gIta- Govinda* of Jayadeva of the 12th century.

Starting from Jnaneswar of the 13th century, the Maharashtrian tradition brought forth a philosophy which in some sense unified the two paths of *jnAna* and bhakti. According to this school, the ultimate Brahman is both attributeless and attributed – that is, both impersonal and personal. To reach the Personal Ultimate one needs the bhakti of Love. To reach the Formless Ultimate one needs Enlightenment. For the former there is any one of nine methods which are classical.

To reach the Impersonal Ultimate one needs to discipline oneself through the three-fold ascent of *SravaNa* (listening), *manana* (deliberation on what has been learnt) and *nididhyAsanA* (the analysis and synthesis of the accrued knowledge). This school has a stronghold in the Maharashtra area because of a succession of great devotees and expositors like *Namdev* (13th and 14th centuries) Eknath (16th century), Tukaram (17th century) and Samarth Ramdas (also of the 17th century)

CHAPTER 13

A Quick Overview of the Gita

The attitude of detachment is the essential core of what goes by the name of karma yoga, the yoga of selfless, dedicated action. This attitude is the lesson that philosophy teaches us. From the innumerable stories of the *purANas* and our everyday experience, we note that whenever, for instance, there is an irresoluble dilemma in life, death or its equivalent, we tend to philosophize. This resort to philosophy is not for a psychological satisfaction, nor is it an attempt at helpless compromise with reality. It is in fact the only means to get to the root of the matter. In the classical case where Arjuna presents his dilemma to Krishna on the battlefield and collapses, the first thing that Krishna does is to recall to him the nature of the Atman. Krishna says: 'You are grieving about something that ought not to be grieved about, neither these kith and kin of yours nor you as Arjuna are everlasting'. 'Go about in the world', says Krishna, 'fully conscious of the fact that you are the Atman, and therefore you can never be tarnished by these feelings of joy and sorrow, pleasure and pain, friendship and enmity. Be completely detached as if you were an actor on the stage. An actor does not hesitate to 'kill' his bosom friend who is playing the part of the enemy on the stage'. 'Detachment' does not imply ineffectiveness as some critics would have it. Only when you are completely detached can you do a job without being confused by excitement. This does not mean that you are not involved. Certainly you are. As an actor on the stage you have to be involved with everything that goes on there and especially with the part you play; and you must play it well. Even if you have to be angry on the stage, you have to be; but the real You - whatever you are outside the stage - is not angry. This is karma yoga. You are acting in the world according to the role given to you, according to your *sva-dharma* (= one's own duty), and performing it effectively, never for a moment forgetting the fact, that it is your duty to act without expecting anything out of it. The thief in the play who is stealing currency notes (real notes, that is) can never for a moment believe that the currency will stay with him, the real him!. So the *gIta* says: 'Do your duty, don't be attached to the outcome thereof.'

What does it mean 'not to be attached'? The *gItA* describes what happens after 'attachment'. *(bhagavad-gItA: 2- 62, 63):*

> *sangAt-samjAyate kAmah*
> *kAmAt-krodho'bhijAyate /*
> *krodhAd-bhavati sammohaH*

sammohAt-smRti-vibhramah /
smRtibramshAd-buddhi-nAshaH
buddhi nAshAt-praNashyati //

Anxious desire follows attachment; the non-fulfillment of that desire leads to anger; only one step away is delusion, followed by a confusion of intellect; and this leads to the failure of intellect; and thereafter, disaster.

The effort therefore should be to overcome these consequences of attachment and that is what one means by 'not to be attached'. If a person can go about one's duties for the sake of duty and not claim authorship, ownership or doership for oneself then one will not be subject to the experience of resultant pleasure or pain. Neither the good results nor the bad results of his actions would bind him. So long as any actions bind him he has to return to the cycle of transmigration. The ultimate purpose is to see that neither the good nor the bad keeps us in bondage. That is why we are advised to be detached.

Total detachment does not mean asceticism. Poverty is not the only gateway to purity. Asceticism usually is taken to mean retiring to the forest and seeking in the serenity of the silence there a communion with the divine. This is certainly a worthwhile goal but this is not prescribed for the millions who cannot but toil in the humdrum world of *samsAra*. Hinduism has different prescriptions for different levels of seekers. Retiring to the forest as an ascetic is prescribed for those who are ready for the fourth stage of life. For the millions of us, when the scriptures say 'be detached' they mean 'have a detached attitude'. It is the attitude that matters, not the physical act of renuciation. The physical act of renunciation, if it is not simultaneously accompanied by the complete cessation of the feeling of attachment to anything that binds, is only hypocrisy *(gItA, 3 - 6):*

> ***karmendriyANi samyamya ya Aste manasA smaran /***
>
> ***indriyArthAn vimUDhAtmA mithyAcAras-sa ucyate //***

The one of deluded understanding who, restraining the organs of action, sits thinking in his mind of the sense objects, is called a hypocrite.

On the other hand, being in the world, if you go about its affairs with a feeling of detachment, that is exactly what is wanted of a seeker who is a householder. Karma yoga recognizes that the real evil is not in the physical possessions themselves but in the attachment to them. It is not the ordinary duties involved in the process of earning a livelihood that should be abhorred, but selfishness - which is a consequence of attachment to the non Self. It is this that should be suppressed and ultimately conquered. It is in this sense that Krishna advises Arjuna to fight the battle rather than show attachment and compassion to his fellow-men and retire. Krishna makes a remarkable statement in this strain, which must be engraved in gold: (Gita, 3-30):

mayi sarvANi karmANi sanyasy-AdhyAtma-cetasA /

nirAshir-nirmamo bhUtvA yudhyasva vigata- jvaraH //

Renouncing all actions unto Me, with the mind centred on the Self, without any desire and without any ego, go and fight, without any fever (of excitement).

It is significant to note that one has to 'fight' without desire, without ego and without excitement! When interpreted for the common man this means: Do carry on your life's journey doing all your duties without selfishness, without the fever and excitement that you normally show in chasing happiness and satisfaction. How is this possible? It should be made possible. That is karma yoga.

For this it may not be necessary (though advantageous) to go along the path of religious belief, involving an acceptance of the divinity of man, the conviction that there is a supreme power, that the authority of the scriptures is unquestionable, and so on. All that is required is the belief in the dignity of man. Thus one may encounter a staunch karma yogi who does not believe in God and religion. Such a karma yogi will do his duties devotedly, not because he will otherwise incur demerit but because he knows no other way to be of use to himself and to society. Social responsibilities will be meticulously discharged by him because he is convinced that he owes service to society for his very sustenance as a member of that society. He believes that each one of us must do his or her job sincerely and to the best of one's ability. If the returns of work do not properly match the amount of effort expended and the efficiency and dedication with which it is executed, he knows that these ills of society can never be corrected by rebellion. But he is not a conformist. He might well be an unusual person who has struck out a new path for service to society, and in following it exhibits zeal and steadfastness. Such a karma yogi has no ambitions for himself except some residual attachment for the work he is doing and he would, therefore not yield to anybody in estimating the importance of his work

This kind of social action, without any self-interest is a simple way of training oneself in karma yoga. It is in fact the first thing that young people must learn. Identifying oneself with a cause, with a social purpose, one gets attracted by the charms and thrills of social service and the innate satisfaction it provides. Such social service done as a dedication to society without the least self-interest, and in a totally detached attitude of self-effacement, such action goes by the fascinating name of *yajna,* in Hinduism.

The word *yajna,* is one of those words from Hindu religion and spirituality which has no English equivalent. Roughly, it means sacrifice, either ritualistic in the conventional sense of Hindu orthodoxy, or a devotional act without an egocentric attachment. In a broader sense, any action done for the good of others, done with dedication and without desire or expectation or attachment or selfishness may be called a *yajna*. Here 'dedication' means 'voluntary acceptance of suffering for the benefit of others'. The concept is elaborately dealt with in the third chapter of the *gItA*. The central purport is as follows.

When one acts, one has to take responsibility for the good or bad effects of the action. Dexterity in action *(karmasu kaushalaM)* according to the *gItA,* is that manner of involvement in action in which the effects do not bind one in terms of *AgAmi* karma. Only when one has desire for the fruits thereof, is one bound by the implications of one's action. When one performs an action because it is one's duty to do it, as for example, when a judge sentences a criminal to death, the results of the action do not bind the judge. The judge does not incur any sin meting out a death sentence as part of his duty. This is *yajna*. The *gItA* urges that every action must be done in a spirit of *yajna*. That is the way to be involved in action and at the same time be free from the bondage of action, the ultimate aim being the eradication of all *vAsanAs,* which are quality-imprints of thoughts and actions of the past including all previous lives, left in the subconscious.

Both good and bad, from the mind-complex, one has to discover the right way to act in the living world, a way which does not result in the accumulation of further *vAsanAs*. The initial attempt in one's journey should be to avoid accumulating bad *vAsanAs,* that is, to stay away from sinful acts. To live in subservience to the calls and appetites of the outer world is the origin of all sins. Such subservience contributes to 'inhuman' and 'undivine' *vAsanAs* piling up in the mind. From *vAsanAs* to thoughts and from thoughts to actions is a very familiar chain. To break it, one has to substitute the evil *vAsanAs* by divine *vAsanAs* which arise out of *puNya-karma*, the karma which arises out of compassion and dedicated devotion to the divine and the universal brotherhood of man. This substitution is not a simple process. One may think of the mind-complex as a large reservoir of *vAsanAs,* the contents of which cannot be poured out. So in order to 'substitute' good *vAsanAs* for bad ones, all one can do is really to 'pour' more and more good *vAsanAs* into the reservoir and dilute its badness.

Punya karmas will create *vAsanAs* which will gradually overwhelm the pattern of sin that exists in the mind. The *gItA* gives us a clear recipe for exactly this breaking of the *vAsanA*-thought-action chain which takes us down the scale of *samsAra*. The *gItA* says: 'Do your assigned duty and do it in the spirit of *yajna'*. That is, do your duty because you have to do it. It is not important to do what you want to do but rather it is important to begin to like to do what you have to do. Do it without desire. Do it as if it were a part you have to play and you have no stake in your part. The real stakes are beyond the play. Within the play one should have no desire or attachment. This is the spirit of *yajna*.

The quality of a 'doer' of actions has been classified by the *gItA* in the standard three-fold way. The lowest type of 'doer' has no control (*ayuktaH*) over himself. He is unsteady in his application. His low instincts and impulses prod him on to behave in a vulgar (*prAkRta*) way. And he becomes dishonest (*shaTaH*) and so unbending (*stabdhaH*) that he is stubborn in his errors and obstinate in his stupidity. He is bent upon creating quarrels and disputes and so the world knows him to be malicious (*naishkRtikaH*). Avoiding all creative endeavours, productive or purposeful, he is a model of indolence (*alasaH*). Consequently he becomes unable to meet life's challenges and so is despondent (*vishhAdI*). Naturally he postpones (*dIrgha-sUtrI*) everything until it is too late. Such a person is called a *tAmasa-kartA: (gItA, 18 -28):*

ayuktaH prAkRtaH
stabdhaH shaTo naishkRtiko'lasaH /
vishAdI dIrgh-sUtrI ca

kartA tAmasa ucyate //

No student, for instance, would like to belong to this category either in his student-life or afterwards. We all know what it means to be a good student. We think that it is the type of work, described as that of the better 'doer' (that is, better than the one classified as *tAmasa-kartA*) described in the *gItA* itself, the doer who is called a *rAjasic* (=dynamic, passionate) doer. *gItA 18 - 27:*

> *rAgI karma-phala-prepsuH*
> *lubdho himsAtmako'SuciH /*
> *harsha-shokAnvitaH kartA*
>
> *rAjasaH parikIrtatah /*

Passionate, desiring to gain the fruits-of-actions, greedy, harmful, impure, full of delight and grief,

Such a person is constantly thinking of this reward or that result of his performance. Full of joy in success or of grief in failure, he is the typical restless teenager who is the fertile ground for all the ambitions of that age. The world thinks of such a student as the right kind, since the general opinion is: how else can a student behave? We think that he has to be a go- getter, he has to be dynamic, pushing, aggressive, motivated by the carrots of rewards for his actions.

But even here, when we project the ideas of karma yoga and the concept of dedication, the intelligent student himself gets genuine doubts as to whether such a one-upmanship is right. Let us be more specific. Consider the situation of a teenager, a university student living away from his parents or guardians, in a hostel or dorm in the environment of a student population well-known for its dynamism, its restlessness, for a mixture of both narrow as well as sophisticatedly broad aims, and for its almost rudderless groping through this competitive world of aggression and one-up-manship. What is the norm for such a person in terms of right action? This is a question that constantly confronts young people because sharply conflicting pictures are presented to them by the 'adult' world of opportunism, camouflaged by a coating of fair play and justice. They very often see the tragic picture of so-called righteousness, expressed in the form of exhibitionist devotion, coexistent with a deep undercurrent of selfishness and dishonesty. Modern youth are in a dilemma. Their own educational ambitions seem selfish to them as they get ideas, prematurely perhaps, for reforming the world and taking leadership in their own hands. A student's svadharma is to study, but a student with a superficial view of religion mistakenly believes that to concentrate on one's studies and try to score over one's fellow students is a selfish pursuit and so it encourages the very ego which religious spirituality decries.

To such a student the Gita says: Do your duty in the spirit of *yajna* and do not be attached to the fruits of your efforts. You may ask: 'If I am not attached to the result of my examinations then with what motivation do I study?'. When the *gItA* says: 'Do not be attached', it means 'Do not have illusions, false expectations about the fruits of actions, anxieties concerning the results and fears of future calamities that have not yet happened'. All these are consequences of attachment. When you sit down to study for examinations, if, instead of studying, you keep thinking about what is likely to be the nature of the question paper in the examination, what is the likelihood that so-and-so may do better than you, what will happen if you do not do well, what minimum effort you have to put in so that you may scrape through the examination, and so on, then you have allowed your attachment to the results of the examination to dominate your thinking. This is precisely what karma yoga wants you to avoid. It says: 'Do your duty in a spirit of dedication'. You may ask: 'What is the meaning of dedication in the context of my daily chore of studies? To whom do I dedicate myself? Why? What is the outcome of such dedication? How does it alter the picture?' It does; how it does so we will now understand through an example.

Think of your mother at home, far away; she is looking forward to your returning from college with a feather in your academic cap. She expects you to follow certain norms in your daily activities and she has great hopes about your returning to her more balanced, more mature, more knowledgeable, than when she sent you to college. You certainly do not want to disappoint her. Now comes the crucial technique of *yajna*. It says, for example, 'Dedicate all your actions to your mother, do everything because your mother would like you to do it that way. Avoid certain things because your mother would want you to do so'. In short, you live and act as your mother would want you to. In other words you have dedicated your every step to your mother. Dedication is the voluntary acceptance of suffering for another's sake and, in this case, for your mother's sake, that is, if you think being a good student for your mother's sake is a suffering. This is the karma yoga of the student who has dedicated all his actions to his beloved mother. The consequences of such a dedication must be seen to be believed. At almost every step one experiences an alchemy taking place in one's mind; a constant war will be waged in the inner recesses of the mind between the good *vAsanAs* and the not-so-good *vAsanAs* and each time the conviction that one is doing things for the sake of one's mother at home will gradually resolve issues and tilt them towards the side of the better *vAsanAs*. Such a student may be said to be doing *svAdhyAya-yajna*, the *yajna* of study.

This is exactly what the *gItA* describes in its classification of 'doer' as 'satvic' (the ideally noble) in *gItA 18-26:*

mukta-sango-naham-vAdI
dhRty-utsAha-samanvitaH /
siddhy-asiddhyor-nirvikAraH

kartA sAtvika ucyate //

Free from attachment, free from egoism, full of a fixed impersonal resolution and a calm rectitude of zeal, unelated by success and undepressed by failure, such a one is called the *sAtvika-kartA*.

This verse being the punchline in our elaboration of the *yajna* attitude, we treat the concepts one by one in detail.

Free from attachment: This is easier said than done. The scriptures with one voice give the recipe how to be free from attachment. The human mind by nature cannot obey the commandment of non-attachment. Therefore they say, attach yourself to God. The Tamil *tirukuRaL* puts this most succintly and beautifully:

paRRuga paRRaRRAn paRRinai appaRRaip-

parruga parru viDaRku /

Acquire only the attachment to God who has no attachment Himself. In order to get rid of all attachments that attachment has to be acquired.

This is the religious facet of karma yoga. In the modern terminology of Psychology this is called 'releasing from worldly ties by retying to Spirit'. But this attitude would require a belief in God and things of the 'beyond'. Youth may perhaps want a prop without the intervention of the idea of God. The mother as a deity of dedication is only one example of how karma yoga can be implemented even at the level of a teen-age student and even for the purpose of what appears to be a most self-centred action in which the good of the society does not enter the picture and wherein only the good of one's own self is the prime mover. The mystery of the *yajna* attitude is its conversion of even an act of selfishness into an act of dedication and detachment! So the student, in tune with his attitude of dedication to his mother, should see to it that attachment to his mother replaces his perennial attachment to the results of his work. For a man in (incidentally, not 'of') the world, this means he is either attached to his God whom He serves or to his abstract God of Service – which may be either the society, the cause, or the organization he serves. In all cases there is attachment no doubt but the attachment is never for an end which is self-centred. This is the *yajna* attitude. In the secular world this means one is stepping clear of bonds and physically moving away from problems so that even difficult problems of management or tricky personal problems get solved from a distance.

Free from egoism. Again the dedication takes care of this. Whether it is the Marketing Executive, the Administrative Manager, the student on the climb, or the man in the world, the dedication to either the cause, or the organization, or the mother, or God, is the proper antidote for curtailing the ego and in due time making it totally subservient to everything else. Once the ego is put in its place, the *yajna* attitude is on.

They are put in here as the necessary associates of an ideal doer, they show that a work done with healthy detachment is not a work which is indifferently done or something which is executed as an unwanted evil necessity. One enjoys doing the work. And one does it efficiently. It is the spirit with which one does the work rather than the mundane carrots that bring the joy.

Unelated by success and undepressed by failure: Here it is that the student will know what it is to dedicate his work to his mother. It is common knowledge that when a child does not perform in school it is the father, (generally), more than the mother, who will be uncompromising. The mother usually takes the stand that the child did its best and she hopes for a better performance in the future. The dedication to the mother by the teen-age student of all his work, both its success and its failure, achieves two things. First, it takes off the sting of the performance (positive or negative) from the student. Secondly the mother is prepared to take the disappointment of the failure better. In the general case of the man in the world, the success and failure would not be taken personally as to cause excitement either way, because one knows by his dedication to the Cause or the God, that one has done the best under the circumstances.

The alchemy of the *yajna* attitude of even ordinary acts to a larger cause, be it as concrete as one's mother at home, or as unsubstantial as God in heaven, or as abstract as any impersonal noble cause, has to be experienced to be believed. It confirms the recurring emphasis in the scriptures on the importance of correct attitudes. Therefore it is the attitude with which you approach your karma that is important, rather than the karma itself. It is precisely this train of argument that Lord Krishna uses in urging Arjuna to fight and not to retreat. Arjuna is immersed in the disease of false identification with the eternal world of 'his' kith and kin, says Krishna. Neither they nor he are permanent everlasting entities and so there is no sense in crying over the possible death of what is destined to die. If he identified himself with his Self, which is what he ought to do, then neither the heat and cold of the external world nor the alternatives of pleasure and pain of the mental world would affect him. His right is only to the action and not to the results thereof. Equanimity concerning success or failure is the yoga for him. Not to retreat from a war already declared is the *svadharma* of the Kshatriya that he is. If he thinks that retreating to solitude, renouncing the world, would give him peace, he is mistaken – for, the attitude with which he renounces is the deciding factor. If the attitude is not that of a *jnAni* who has attained enlightenment, but is that of an emotionally charged warrior whose compassion for his kith and kin has got the better of him, then such a meolodramatic withdrawal from the world would not bring peace; for the mind would continue to be in turmoil in the vortex of its worldly attachments. It does not have the maturity of dispassion that should precede renunciation. Doing what is assigned to one as one's duty is far more honourable than running away from action in dislike of that action. If one does one's duty in the spirit of yajna, the actions do not bind one.

The whole universe, says Krishna, is a complex of mutual *yajnas*. When the world was re-created by the Lord at the beginning of the *kalpa,* He created divine beings to be in charge of the elements and ordained that human beings should propitiate these gods to ensure that the elements behave properly. These *yajnas* thus give rise to a complex ecological cycle. *Yajna* sustains the normal behaviour of the elements. The latter in turn sustains the fertility and usefulness of the environment in which we live, which sustains humanity, whose duty it is to perform the different *yajnas* enjoined on them. This cycle started by the Lord at the time of creation cannot be interrupted except at the peril of the collapse of the system itself.

Let us now try to understand the concept of *yajna* as Lord Krishna explains it. He talks in the language of the times, when it was normal to talk about creation, divine beings, *yajnas* to propitiate them, and so on. The concept is difficult to appreciate if one does not have a feel for these ideas which are extra-normal to modern thinking. Modern interpretations are however available and one such is Swami Chinmayananda's. Our productive potential, including labour and capital, says the Swami, has to be propitiated selflessly. Without a generous accommodation to this productive potential in an unselfish manner, without this *yajna,* no society can hope to effectively reap the benefits that can accrue to it from the environment. The principle of detachment from selfish ends is inbuilt in this yajna. The divinity of the elements is the productive potential latent in the richness of Mother Earth and the capabilities of labour and capital. So when Krishna says, 'Do your actions in the spirit of *yajna*' a modern secularly oriented person may take it to mean: 'Do your duty because you are a link, though only one, in that vast chain of the nation's productive potential and you have to do your duty unselfishly, always aware of the rights and needs of the other man, however high or low he may be'. This is the *yajna* of propitiation of the productive potential.

Let us come back to Krishna who is repeatedly asked by Arjuna: 'Which is the correct path - renunciation or the path of action?' But Hinduism does not have binary answers to such questions.

So Krishna naturally extols both the paths and delineates the types of people and the paths which will suit them. One who is in the initial stages of spiritual evolution, one who is a householder, one who is still engrossed in the pursuit of his worldly desires and aspirations, one who is restless and dynamic – for such people the path of action is prescribed. But, for the same person, when he is at a stage where he is established in equanimity, for one who has been able to disentangle himself from the spiralling coils of desires and ever-increasing aspirations, for one who has traversed a long way in the practice of meditation, for one whose tendencies have settled down to a state of calm and quiet – for such people the path of renunciation is prescribed. Action and non-action are opposites, but a proper understanding of both is necessary for the efficient practice of karma yoga.

To see action in non-action and non-action in action is the perception of the wise, says Krishna in *gItA, 4 - 18:*

karmaNyakarma yaH paSyet
akarmaNi ca karma yaH /

sa buddhimAn manushyeshu

As we travel in a train we see the landscape 'moving' in the opposite direction and have a feeling, which it is particularly the privilege of innocent children to cherish, that the moving train is actually stationary. Carrying this analogy over to the Self which is ever fixed and stationary, we feel, ignorant as we are, that the entire world is moving around us, fully active and dynamic, and it appears that the world is full of action. Actually it is our mind that projects itself on the objects of the universe and makes them exist in the first place. But for the mind, but for the Eternal Divine principle behind it, none of the worlds we know through our senses would exist. Only brahman persists, all-pervading, still without motion, because an all-pervasive entity cannot have motion; there is no space for it to move ! So the wise man sees non-action in all the turmoil around him. And, for the same reason, to attribute non-action to the Self which stands still as it were is only to comprehend the Self relatively. It is the Self which permeates everywhere, which is the substratum of everything that we see and which is the prime mover par excellence. The Self, therefore, is the chief agent of action, as it were, though it appears to be a silent witness, uninvolved in the noise and turbulence of the external world. it is in this sense that the wise man sees action in non-action.

Thus Reality cannot be put into watertight pigeonholes and described as only this and not that. Action and non-action are relative concepts. When the whole world is awake and full of activity, for the enlightened man who ceases to be involved in it, it is the calm of the night, to borrow the imagery of the gItA. When the whole world is ignorant of the presence of the Cosmic Power and is therefore asleep, it is the Wise Enlightened Being who is awake; for Him the Absolute Light is radiating with all its brilliance and it is he who is enjoying the permanent bliss of wisdom and light.

yA nisha sarva-bhUtAnAm tasyAM jAgarti
samyamI

yasyAM jagrati bhUtAni sA niSa paSyato
muneH //

So who is asleep, who is awake? Hindu literature abounds in such contrasts. The rhetoric of the presentation is only to bring home to us the relative nature of every experience. Karma Yoga therefore derives its strength and sanction from a thorough understanding of what is everlasting and what is transient.

A karma yogi goes about the world in the full awareness that the action he performs pertains to the external world to which he is duty bound to respond, whereas his Internal Self is totally unaffected by anything that happens to his physical or mental self. He is happy within himself, having cast off the desires arising in his mind. Neither desire nor fear nor anger can upset him. He is not overwhelmed by grief nor is he excited by pleasure. He receives experiences as they come - be they plesurable or sorrowful. The one does not enthuse him nor the other depress him,. Just as a tortoise withdraws his head and all its limbs under its shell, he withdraws his sense organs from their objects of enjoyment. Having seen the Absolute, he has no taste for the trivialities of sense perception. Such a person goes about the world desireless, rid of all egoistic concepts of mine and thine, ever peaceful and happy. He is called a *sthita-prajna,* one of firm wisdom. It is the description of this ecstatic stage of human experience that prompts Arjuna to ask again and again whether he should not therefore withdraw from action. The answer comes, as we have seen, in the form of a paradox. He who physically runs away for fear of involvement has not really run away because his egoism has taken hold of him. But *he who is still in the world but does his duty with an attitude of total detachment is the one who has really renounced the world.*

To sum up, karma yoga is selfless desireless action – action, for all purposes, done exactly as would be done by a person who is totally involved and attached. The difference is only in the mental attitude of the doer. Service to society done this way is Service to God. Service to elders, parents and ancestors is a duty in which one engages oneself not for reward but for the discharge of an obligation or debt. *NishkAma- karma* (desireless action) performed in this way leads to the purification of the mind. *VAsanAs*, imprinted in the mind for ages, can be eradicated only by desireless action. Give all you can but never ask for the fruit.

The attitude of doing one's duty for its own sake is the heritage of Hindu culture, handed down from generation to generation. Even those Hindus who are not educated or scholarly, even those who come from very deprived environments, understand this concept. The rationale of all this lies in the fact that even an apparently imperfect or faulty action does not contaminate one when it is done without any desire or selfishness. No action, for that matter, is perfect. Imperfections will always be there in any action. But the imperfect element will not affect the doer if he is totally unselfish. We have already cited the example of a judge sentencing a criminal to death. Another dramatic example is that of a three-month old infant kicking its mother. Does it leave any *vAsanA* of sin in the doer? On the other hand, if the same child grows into an adult of 20 and now, in ungrateful anger, kicks his mother, there is a difference. The action is the same, but the attitude is different. The one taints the mind and the other does not. This is what our scriptures mean when they say that actions done without selfishness or desire will not bind you. such actions are the summum bonum of karma yoga. To one who believes in the scriptures, gods and the myths associated with them, dedication of all actions to God would come naturally. For instead of arguing about what is detachment, what is non-action and action and so on, all he does is to simply think of God as the director of all his thoughts and deeds and dedicate them to Him. Then the alchemy which we have mentioned earlier takes over and the several imperfections that are bound to have been there in the beginning will all disappear in due time and karma yoga will then become a second nature. And then, and only then, will every action performed by him be a *yajna.*

CHAPTER 14

Logic of Advaita Part 1

Of the three paths to perfection, namely, Karma (Action), Bhakti (Devotion) and Jnana (Knowledge), the third one, *jnAna yoga*, is the most difficult, even to explain. It is prescribed particularly for highly evolved intellects. In fact, people who can practise *jnAna yoga* form such a small group that it is not practicable to draw analogies and examples from everyday experiences to help describe and understand it. When one reaches this stage of enlightenment one is far from the general run of humanity. The multiplicity of everyday human experience is left far behind. What happens at that stage is open to debate and has in fact been described in not necessarily identical ways by great scholars who are known to have had first-hand experience of it.

To understand Hinduism in its totality, some understanding, vague though it may turn out to be, of at least one major school of Hindu religious philosophy is essential. The common Hindu masses, who have carried forward the torch of the religion from time immemorial might not be able either to understand fully or communicate even partly the principles of Hindu philosophy, but any knowledgeable and careful observer will recognise that their beliefs and attitudes can be traced back to one or other of the great schools of Hindu philosophy. It is as if there were a multidimensional perspective in which the nature of totality must be viewed, but individuals are each one-dimensional in their intellectual perspective and each sees only what is projected in his dimension. He would never understand where the visual impression, as is reflected in his one-dimensional experience, comes from. When Hindu philosophers tell him that it is such and such a spiritual context that brings about what he experiences, he thinks they are bringing in spirituality unnecessarily. Actually, what is happening is that he lives in the one-dimensional projection of the totality that is not revealed to him in his physical experience. If he is sufficiently intelligent and motivated he can mentally rise from his one-dimensional limitation and comprehend the Universe in its totality. This is the purpose of studying and learning about *jnAna Yoga*. The practice of it is then the next step in one's spiritual ascent.

Different masters give seemingly different accounts of what totality is. Any attempt by us to debate which of them is right would be futile, for, while the discussion is carried on in terms of intellectual analysis, it does not end there. The conclusions drawn from this analysis have to be corroborated by actual personal experience. Not many return from that experience to tell us what they realized. It is given only to a Buddha, a Shankara, a Ramanuja, a Ramakrishna or an Aurobindo to be able to tell us what they 'saw'. Even though these explanations and interpretations differ in their details, what each of them means to us when they are projected to the one-dimensional phenomenality of our worldly experience is identical. <u>That is why Hinduism is one religion in spite of the so-called plurality of interpretations of the Vedas and Upanishads.</u> As such, it does not matter which of the schools of philosophy one follows or is convinced about – it is only a matter of outlook and taste. So far as the layman is concerned, the scholarliness of the debate about the correctness or otherwise of any of the schools of philosophy is not relevant. What matters is the attempt to get a glimpse of the beauty and profundity of ideas that constitute these philosophies. Keeping this background in mind, we shall take up Shankara's way of looking at *jnAna yoga,* what may be called *advaita yoga* – the Yoga of Non-duality. We shall also touch upon the credibility aspect in order to stabilise one's *shraddhA* (faith).

Morality, fair play, ethics, justice, and duty are the basis of karma yoga. Faith, conviction and an attitude of surrender are the basis of bhakti yoga. But just as morality is not the end aim of religion, ecstatic yearning for the Grace of God is only a means, not an end. However close a devotee may feel to communion with God, there is always a distance that persists between God and Man, and so long as this distance exists, says Shankara, you have not reached the goal. Karma Yoga may be termed an attempt at ethical ascent towards this goal, towards the ideal from the actual. Bhakti yoga, may, in similar terms, be described as a religious ascent towards the perfect God by an imperfect Soul. In *jnAna yoga,* however, there is no such duality between the ideal and the actual or between the perfect and the imperfect. In the ascent of bhakti we experience only a fragment of the grandeur of God, but in *jnAna,* when the eyes of wisdom are opened, He is seen as He really is and not as what He is in relation to the universe. The grandeur that is God is revealed in all its totality of magnificence, and realization dawns that all our boasted knowledge of Him so far was only ignorance.

This does not mean that God is really unknowable. One of the beauties of Hinduism is that it teaches us that, while God is infinitely higher than ourselves, He is also infinitely near to us. He is nearer to us than our hands and feet. He is the Soul of our souls. He is the one that survives in us from childhood to adulthood and through old age, from birth, as the I that we talk of when we refer to ourselves (7th shloka of *Dakshinamurthi ashtakam* of Shankara, beginning with *bAlyAdishvapi*). He is neither the body nor the senses, nor the mind nor the ego, nor the intellect; He is the I that is none of these, but is far distant from anything that we can call ours in a related manner like spouse, issue, wealth, possessions and so forth (1st shloka of *Advaita-pancharatnam* of Shankara beginning with *'nAhaM deho'*). He is the ever-present witness to all our experiences. He is really our Atman.

He is Brahman. He is the One Reality beyond which there is none. Brahman and Atman differ, if at all, only in our approach. Atman is the name given to the highest Reality if we seek one such within ourselves. Brahman is the name given to the highest Reality if we seek one such in the universe. The greatest revelation of the Upanishads is the essential identity between Brahman (also denoted by the word *paramAtman)* and Atman (also known by the word *jIvAtman,* or the soul) as revealed by the grand mystic pronouncements called the *mahAvAkyas* of the four Vedas. Once the identity is established, the two terms become interchangeable and it makes no difference whether we speak of the Absolute of the Upanishads as Brahman or Atman.

But even though Godhead is so near to all of us, it is very difficult to realise Him. This is because we have to cease to be ourselves before we can know Him as He is. The difficulty in this concept is the fact that God is both transcendent and immanent. The immanence aspect is inbuilt into the concept of Atman and the transcendence aspect in the concept of Brahman. The scriptures, particularly the Upanishads and the Gita share with us their dilemma in having to describe both these aspects simultaneously. They adopt one of two alternatives. On the one hand they use the superlatives of all the qualities they can think of:

It is smaller than the smallest, bigger than the biggest, it is that which is supreme, than which there is nothing higher, than which there is nothing more minute, than which there is nothing more comprehensive (*MahAnArAyanopanishd - aNoraNIyAn)*).

He strides the entire universe, He is the purest of the pure, most auspicious of all that is auspicious, the God of Gods, the Imperishable Father of all Beings. (*pavitrANAm pavitraM yo* – Preliminary shlokas to *Vishnu Sahasranama*).

On the other hand they use negation of all the finite things that we are capable of expressing:

Whatever cannot be indicated by speech but that motivates all speech, that is Brahman; whatever cannot be seen by the eyes, but by which the eye sees, that is Brahman; not that which is worshipped *(Kenopanishad: yadvAcA anabhyuditam... 1-5; yaccakshushA na pashyati -1-7)*;

Neither internal consciousness nor external consciousness nor both; not a bundle of consciousness either; not the conscious One nor the non-conscious One; cannot be perceived, cannot be related, cannot be handled, cannot be attributed, cannot be indicated, nor can it be an object of thought *(Mandukyopanishad 7: nAntaH pragyam)*

When the scriptures use negatives like these we should not take them to mean that Brahman is just a complete negation. It only means that our finite expressions can never do full justice to the infinite grandeur that is God, that God is wholly other than what we know in the world. He is the unifying principle behind all creatures. He is the canvas on which we shine as painted pictures.

About such an ineffable perfection that is God the only thing we may predicate is that IT EXISTS. It is perfect and pure spirit, pure knowledge. Brahman is not an object of knowledge in the sense that we have objects of knowledge in our everyday experience. 'Atman cannot be obtained by just study or learned discussion; It comes to one who yearns for Realization and whose mind has learnt to look for it within himself' (*Kenopanishad*). 'All this world is permeated by *paramAtman*; they all abide in Him. But He stands apart.' (B.G.VII -4). 'Everything in the universe abides in the Supreme Being' (*Ishopanishad*). The objects of our everyday experience are presented to our sense perceptions and they are 'objects' in relation to a knowing 'subject'. But Brahman cannot be known this way. Brahman is Truth, Knowledge, Infinitude. ('*satyam, jnAnaM, anantaM*': *Taittiriyopanishad*). It is the Truth of Truths (*Bhagavatam X-2-26*). If it 'knows' something the act of knowing has changed its status and this is contradictory to its nature, namely, *satyaM. JnAnaM* therefore means not mere knowledge but consciousness itself. It is the Absolute Consciousness we are talking about here, where there is nothing else to be conscious of. <u>Just as light is light even if there is nothing to be lighted, so also is Consciousness.</u> Brahman is the one Reality which is unchanging, unlimited, without a second and is consciousness itself. 'He who thinks he knows, really thereby proves he is ignorant. He who realizes that he does not know Him has best understood Him' (*Kenopanishad*). Thus Brahman is not an object of understanding in the ordinary sense and it follows that the categories of understanding, such as cause and effect, substance and attribute, have no bearing so far as Brahman is concerned. Knowledge of Brahman is not derived in the usual way, by observation and experiment, but by personal experience, insight and realization. 'To know Brahman is to become Brahman' is the classical refrain of the Upanishads. It is a deep communion, what Shankara calls direct realization (*aparokshAnubhuti*).

According to Shankara, therefore, Brahman is *nirguNa* (attributeless and non-relational). You can't relate it to something and make a statement out of it. The world of difference is not a manifestation of *NirguNa* Brahman but only its appearance. The appearance is less real than the substratum that contains it. Brahman is the ultimate Reality. The universe belongs to a lower order of reality. Shankara does not deny the multiplicity of the world of experience; he only assigns it to a lower order of reality. *NirguNa* Brahman is therefore so unique that nothing on this side of experience, however sublime or elevating, can approximate to it. Attempting to describe it is like attempting to describe sweetness to someone who has never tasted sweetness. Nothing that the human mind can think of can be affirmed of Brahman.

When one attains communion with it one becomes speechless. 'It is not this', 'It is not that' – this is all that one can say about it. Shankara in giving a name to this philosophy does not call it monism (*ekatva*) – but *advaita* (the philosophy of 'that which has no second'). The term monism gives the impression that it has been achieved by reducing one of two terms placed in opposition to each other. It cannot be characterized as the One, because this has no meaning except in relation to the many. Any other positive characterization will be equally open to this objection. Hence Shankara's description of it as non- dualism. It is not an identity in relation to differences, not a one in relation to the many, not a whole in relation to the parts, not a substance in relation to its attributes, not a cause in relation to the effect. All these are relational concepts and so have to be rejected. The statement that Brahman rises above thought and word should not, however, be interpreted to mean that it is empty and non-existent. The denial of predicates affects only the 'whatness' of the judgement and leaves the 'thatness' untouched. The negation of appearances will not in the least affect the underlying reality.

The concept of different orders of Reality is strictly due to Shankara. It is based on the rising levels of our experience. If something is perceived by one individual, even for a brief moment, it must be granted to be that far real. But the criterion of ultimate reality is that of non-contradiction. To begin with we have illusions and dream experiences. A rope mistaken for a snake, nacre mistaken for silver, the trunk of a tree mistaken for a thief, these are familiar experiences. These objects last only so long as their perception lasts. They suffer contradiction when a higher level of experience – an experience that lasts longer – takes possession of the mind. This reality which vanishes at a higher level of experience is said to be a phenomenal reality and it is known in technical parlance as *prAtibhAsika sattA*. The world which we experience belongs to a higher order of reality called empirical reality (*vyAvahArika sattA*). But even this world is not absolutely real as it is subsumed in a still higher experience. When the fundamental unity of the Self with Brahman is realized, the world of our waking moments is submerged. So Brahman-Consciousness is of a higher order of reality. There is no higher reality beyond that because it is Pure Consciousness. Absence of consciousness is a contradiction in terms. The very knowledge of absence of consciousness implies the existence of some consciousness. This highest intuition which should not be called consciousness of the Absolute, is Consciousness itself. This is the Absolute Ultimate Reality – *pAramArthika sattA*. At this level the dualism of subject and object is no longer present and there is only the mystic communion, which is called *nirvikalpa samAdhi*

What hears sound is the ear. What tastes an edible is the tongue. But both sensations are received by the brain, registered by the mind and the awareness of both sensations is due to the life-force, the Atman-principle within. This Atman-principle is exactly what Consciousness is. It is a bundle of knowledge. When we switch on a light in a dark room, we see many objects. The same light lights them all. But when the room is empty of objects, the emptiness itself is indicated by the same light. In the same way when the room is dark the darkness is registered in our awareness by the light within us. That light within us is Consciousness. It is the same Consciousness that showed the light to us when the room was lighted.

Of course if we were blind this consciousness would not tell us whether the room is lighted or not. But it would know that this body-mind-intellect does not know whether the room is lighted or not. A dead body in the room would not know whether the room is lighted or not and would not even know that it does not know. Because the dead body is just an inert matter without the presence of consciousness (Atman) in it.

> **Question 1: The dead body also should be Consciousness, because Consciousness as the omnipresent Absolute Reality is everywhere. Why then is it not knowledgeable about the lighting in the room?**

Very legitimate question! Although the Ultimate Self (Consciousness) is present at all times and in all things, it cannot shine in everything. Just as a reflection appears only in polished surfaces, so also the Self shines as Consciousness only in the intellect (Shankara's *Atmabodha*, Verse 17). The intellect (and the mind) has already left the body in the case of a dead body!

Question 2: Is it not illogical to talk about a pure contentless consciousness?

No. We shall borrow an illustration used by M.K. Venkatrama Iyer in his book 'Advaita Vedanta'. From architecture to sculpture, from sculpture to painting, from painting to poetry, from poetry to music, there is a gradual transition from a situation of content-domination to one of form-domination. In architecture brick and mortar occupy the dominant content. This dominance recedes into the background when the sculptor with his chisel produces a whole saga out of just one piece of stone. In painting there is very little physical content, but there is a substantial amount of form that predominates. In poetry by mere words one brings out a whole bundle of meanings, emotions and expressions. Here matter or content is at its lowest and form takes over almost fully. But when we move over to music, there are not even words. By the mere form of music one is enraptured into whatever emotion the composer has designed for you. Music is pure form with no material physical content. If this can happen in art, it can also happen in the description of reality behind the universe where, as we advance in spiritual evolution we pass to higher and higher states of consciousness. Starting from the waking state of consciousness in which we are so full of content that even the consciousness behind it is hidden, we go step by step until we reach the stage where there is no matter but only pure spirit, pure consciousness. Twentieth century Physics tells us that our consciousness is in some intricate way mixed up with the external world. Vedanta declares that there is no mixing up, in the sense that there is only consciousness. There is not even a subject and an object.

CHAPTER 15

Logic of Advaita Part 2

Question 3. When the subject and object disappear, are we not left with a complete blank?

No. Who is the 'We' in the question? That is still the 'subject'. It is a mistake to think that when the series of presentations to consciousness come to an end, there is nothing left behind. Even the statement that there is nothing left behind is a piece of knowledge, presupposing consciousness. In the state of profound sleep without dreams, we do not perceive or feel anything. When we get up from sleep we exclaim that we slept like a log and did not know anything about what went on (even in our own body) when we slept. This reminiscent experience would not have been possible if the state of sleep were a blank. While everything is presented to consciousness and is revealed by it consciousness itself is not presented to anything else. In our own everyday experience suppose we are asked to show light without there being anything (even space!) to light. Can we? So also Consciousness is never an object in relation to a subject. It is that which underlies both subject and object and can manifest itself without any aid. This is the ultimate Reality that transcends the three states of waking, dreaming and sleeping. It is known technically as the *turIyA avasthA* (the fourth state, though it should not be termed a 'state'). One can deny everything external to oneself but cannot deny one's own self. The strength of Shankara's *advaita* lies in the fact that it identifies *NirguNa* Brahman with the Atman, the innermost self of Man, which is never deniable.

Question 4: If *NirguNa* Brahman is the ultimate reality and hence the only Godhead that is supreme, how can one worship it? Is it not a contradiction to say there is nothing other than Brahman and also urge one to worship it? Where is the distinction between the worshipper and the worshipped?

Yes. Brahman is not a thing to be worshipped, because it is attributeless – *nirguNa*. Shankara does not say, worship, or do puja to, the Brahman. Brahman has to be known, realized and merged with. Incidentally, this word, 'merged with' is not the correct way of saying it; we are actually struggling with words here! But this sophistication of knowing and realizing is not for the majority of mortals who cannot but cling to names and forms. When Brahman is given a concrete name and form, we call it Ishvara. Then Brahman becomes *saguNa* – that with attributes. Only a *saguNa* Brahman can be worshipped. That worship is what is called Bhakti.

Question 5: Are there two Brahmans? If there is only one, which is what Advaita proclaims to be true, is it *saguNa or nirguNa?*

The *advaita* contention is that Brahman by itself is *nirguNa*. But if you view it from a human angle, with all your physical and psychological limitations, then Brahman appears to you as *saguNa* brahman. It is the human limitations that make us think in terms of a *saguNa* brahman. The limitations, also called *upAdhis,* are the result of *avidyA* (Ignorance) and are nothing but the physical and mental limitations under which we have to function in life. That the Ultimate is non-dual (and therefore *nirguNa*) there is no question. But to be able to realise it as a fact of experience one has to go through the processes of bhakti of God with form and content, with name and description, with qualities and adjuncts. It is such a God that is given the technical name of *SaguNa* Brahman, in contrast to the formless and nameless Absolute. If we view Brahman through our sensory and intellectual apparatus the original unity of the presentation is broken into subject and object and we become conscious of Brahman with attributes. Any time you circumscribe the ultimate Brahman either by means of a name or form or both, you already have the *saguNa* brahman. You are actually talking of a manifestation of the Absolute Reality. He is the Almighty, the incomparable Supreme of all religions. He is the *saguNa* Brahman of Vedanta. Thus the *advaita* view is that *saguNa* Brahman is a means, in fact, the means, to the ultimate goal of attributeless Brahman. In fact, the twelfth chapter of the Gita begins with Arjuna's question: Is worship to be done of the Unmanifested Brahman or the Manifested Brahman? The Unmanifested Brahman corresponds to *nirguNa* Brahman and the Manifested Brahman to *saguNa* Brahman. The Vedic syllable that indicates the former is *'aum'* also called the *PraNava* and the vedic syllable that indicates the latter is *'iim'* which is called the *'Shakti PraNava'*. It is to this Shakti *PraNava* one surrenders in toto: cf. *'tAM padminIm-IM sharaNam ahaM prapadye'*. It is not possible to surrender to 'aum' because the Absolute Brahman represented by 'aum' is *nirguNa* and so will not admit any duality of action, speech or thought.

When we think of *saguNa* Brahman what we have is consciousness of the Absolute rather than Absolute Consciousness. It is the former consciousness, which, when associated with the soul (*jIva*) is tainted by egoism; it is this which carries the individual-generated *vAsanAs* through successive births by virtue of association with the *jIva* and it is this which is a witness to the three states of consciousness, namely, waking, dreaming and sleeping. It is no longer pure spirit but spirit in association with insentient matter. The difference between *saguNa* Brahman and *jIva* the soul is only in respect of the adjuncts (*upAdhis*). So far as the spiritual element is concerned, there is no difference between them. When we think of the limitations as a subjective factor, it is called *avidyA* or ignorance. When we think of them as a cosmic factor, it is cosmic ignorance, technically called *mAyA*. By whatever name we call it, it does not affect Brahman in the least.

MAyA means that which is not absolutely real but which has the power to appear as real. The root word for *mAyA* (pronounced with both vowels long) is maya (pronounced with both vowels short) which has very much to do with magic. Shankara explains *mAyA* as *yA mA sA mAyA*, meaning 'that which is not is *mAyA*'. It is a common misconception that according to Shankara, the world is myth, in fact a total dream, an illusion. Let us examine the word 'dream'. To whom is a dream a dream? Certainly not to the dreamer. The dream is perfectly real to the dreamer. It gets the status of a dream only after the person has awakened from his dream. That the dream is real to the dreamer, nobody denies. Shankara also accepts it, though he calls it, legitimately, apparent reality, or phenomenal reality (*prAtibhAsika sattA*). In fact, the acceptance of the reality of the dream to the dreamer is the king-pin of Shankara's explanation of *advaita*. He bases many of his arguments on the phenomenal reality of the dream. Indeed, one may wonder what else is the value of a dream in God's creation, except to tell us about its unreality compared to the waking state and thereby provide us with the most apt analogy we may have for the relationship between the Absolute Reality of Godhead and apparently concrete experience of the visible universe. This latter is empirical (*vyAvahAric*) reality and it is in between the total unreality or non-existence – *asat* – of the barren mother or of hare's horn and the total reality or absolue truth – *sat* – of Brahman. The dream and similarly the perceptible universe is neither *sat* nor *asat*, therefore, *sad-asad-vilakshana*. It is *mithyA*, meaning, not falsehood, but comparative unreality. When the meaning of '*mithyA*' is thus properly understood, Shankara's classic statement: brahma *satyaM, jagat mithyA* will make the right sense.

MAyA has two powers: the power to conceal the truth and the power to present something else to our perception. The former is called *AvaraNa* Shakti and the latter *vikshepa Shakti*. When we mistake a rope for a snake, the fact that the rope is not visible is due to the *AvaraNa* (concealing) power of *mAyA*. The fact that a snake actually appears to be present, while in reality is not, is due to the *vikshepa* (projecting) power of *mAyA*. It is this dual cosmic power of *mAyA* that brings about the presentation of the physical universe where only Brahman should be cognized.

Questions arise about the ultimate status of *mAyA*. Unless *mAyA* is already present, neither concealment nor projection can take place. Is *mAyA* then coeval with Brahman? Do they exist side by side? Does this not contradict the non-dual status of brahman? Where does *mAyA* operate? What is its base of operation? These questions raise profound issues, which take us to the very core of technical controversies with which the extensive vedantic literature of India is replete. We shall only very briefly touch upon Shankara's bold answers to these questions.

CHAPTER 16

Logic of Advaita Part 3

The base of activity of *mAyA* cannot be brahman because the latter is Absolute Luminosity and there can be no place in it for ignorance or darkness. Nor can the *jIva* be the base of operations of *mAyA*. For *jIva* itself cannot come into existence until *mAyA* has operated. There seems to be an unresolvable logical difficulty here. But the difficulty will vanish once we realise that we are making an implicit assumption which is not valid. <u>We are actually assuming the prior reality of time and space before the appearance of *mAyA*.</u> Otherwise we could not have asked the question: Where does *mAyA* operate? When does it come into existence? These questions are valid only if you have a frame of reference in time and space independent of mAyA. But time and space, points out Shankara, are themselves creations of *mAyA! (cf: mAyA-kalpita-desha-kAla- kalanA vaicitriya chitrIkRRitaM* ... Shloka 2 of Dakshinamurti Ashtakam). Before the universe was made manifest, it was undifferentiated in its cause, brahman, like the sprout in the seed. *mAyA* as grounded in Isvara *(=saguNa brahman),* as an adjunct, posits (= takes as given) conditions such as space and time and produces the variegated world with beings bearing specific names and forms. The question whether *mAyA* as an adjunct of *saguNa brahman* contradicts the principle of non-duality does not arise, for *mAyA* as well as the created world, are *mithyA,* not real. Only if it were a reality besides Isvara there would be duality. The causality of the world which appears in Isvara is structured by the beginningless indeterminable *mAyA* and so the causality is also *mithyA.*

In fact this is also the answer to the physicist's question: When did time originate? Time did not originate in a timeless frame because we would then be begging the question. The very fact that we are conscious of the passage of time is a consequence of *mAyA.* So questions such as, Where does *mAyA* operate? And when did it start operating? are not properly posed. Time and space cannot claim prior existence. It is therefore wrong to ask whether *mAyA* is prior to *jIva* or later than *jIva.* Ultimate Reality is beyond space and time. In the words of Swami Vivekananda, time, space and causation are like the glass through which the Absolute is seen, *but in the Absolute itself, there is neither time, nor space nor causation.* As in the field of modern physics, so in the field of Vedanta, time and space are modes incidental to sense perception and should not be applied to what is trans-empirical. *JIva* and *mAyA* are both given apriori in our experience and we have to take them as such. They are *anAdi* (beginningless). *mAyA* is different from both the real and the unreal. It is in this sense that we say that the world of perception, the common world of experience, cannot be rejected out of hand as totally false, like the hare's horn or the lotus in the sky; nor can it be taken to be totally real, because it suffers contradiction at a higher level of experience.

It is real only in the empirical sense and unreal in the absolute sense.

There is no religion worth talking about without miracles interwoven in its tradition. Miracles are the only phenomena that 'prove' to humanity at large that there is a supreme Power beyond the apparently unquestionable powers of Nature. The very existence of this supreme power though it may be intellectually accepted as a hypothesis never appeals to the heart with the force of a belief through a purely intellectual exercise. On the other hand when you see impossible things happen which simply cannot be explained on any known basis, only then are questions raised in your mind for which the answer has to come from the heart and the mind; for it is the heart by which we mean the emotional part of the mind that then accepts it as a concrete visible proof of divinity, and this results in a firm faith. The life of a Krishna, a Jesus, a Mohammed and a Ramakrishna are full of such impossibilities, which man calls miracles and which cannot be wished out of history. More often than not, only when one discovers some power in a personality which others do not possess, does one start respecting his spirituality. 'Except ye see signs and wonders' says Jesus, 'ye will not believe'. Meet any one who is a close follower of a great saintly leader. You will surely hear them talk enthusiastically about what they consider to be superhuman in their guru, the divine mentor.

A scientist cannot afford to be dogmatic. Miracle is something which goes against any of the known scientific laws. Until the scientist sees the miracle with his own eyes and has tested it under several possible circumstances he would not believe that it happened. Fair enough. But let him not be unscientific enough to say that miracles can never happen. I have known some doctors say in the case of certain unusual emergency cases, 'We have done all that is possible. Let us wait and see. If the patient wakes up well it will certainly be a miracle'. There is no universal law saying 'Everything in the world has to happen only according to scientific laws'. Miracles, for all we know may be the visiting cards of God's presence. The wisdom that one learns from life's experience is sometimes beyond science. Also, 'miracles' rarely repeat themselves or at least do not seem to be repeatable 'at call'. Just because there are frauds in the religious world (the proportion does not seem to be smaller than that in the secular world!) let not the scientist be arrogant enough to assume that he should be able to explain everything. A scientific 'Theory of Everything' is still in the future. When the scientist sees a miracle 'happen' right before his eyes, the most scientific statement that he can truly make is

'It is difficult to believe it. I do not understand it'. That would be the right scientific temper.

A philosopher or an intellectual may reason that there could be an unchanging Atman which is omnipresent, omnipotent and omniscient. He can rise to this level of understanding by successive steps of logical reasoning. A true devotee also understands there is a Supreme Power, *Ishvara*, controller of everything and who is therefore the Supreme Director of Nature. But the vast majority of people are neither philosophers nor intellectuals, nor are they true devotees. They can never comprehend by any amount of logic or intuition that there is a *parAshakti* from which even Nature derives its powers. They believe in God only when that God expresses Himself through things like miracle-healing or other equally miraculous happenings. In fact it is a moot point whether Jesus or Krishna would be held in as much esteem as they are today if their stories were totally devoid of miracles!

All examples of miracles and spiritual wonders – there are hundreds of them in our history, biography, hagiology and literature – only show that when Divinity wills it, there is nothing in this world of science and matter to prevent it from happening the way Divinity wants it. Divine will *(Ishvara-sankalpa)* is sufficient to make things happen, law or no law. It is this *sankalpa* which led to the manifestation of the world from its unmanifested state; in other words, God willed: Let there be creation and there was the primeval creation. We shall leave it to the physicists and other scientists to sort out whether or not He only 'created' the fundamental laws of physics including the quantum laws and allowed the universe including space-time to evolve according to these laws. But Hindu Vedanta is very clear on this point: *mAyA* Shakti the mysterious power of that Supreme Reality, expresses itself when it is divinely so willed!

Belief in the efficacy of *mantra* power is the most common Hindu trait, common to all the votaries of the religion, spread through its multifarious sects and schools. The mantras themselves may differ from sect to sect and school to school. A *mantra* is a vedic hymn, sacrificial formula, a mystical verse or an incantation. In general, it connotes any sacred chant or formula having the power to secure the blessings of God, when lovingly and reverently repeated. One warning has however to be mentioned. One has to respect the rule that no *mantra* would be efficacious unless it is learnt orally from a guru, who has himself that *mantra-siddhi*. By mantra-siddhi, one means that the *mantra* has sufficiently been meditated upon and repeated by the person concerned that the deity of the *mantra* has been realised by the person. The number of times required for this *mantra-siddhi* varies from *mantra* to *mantra*. Very often it goes into several hundreds of thousands. The word *mantra* in Sanskrit means 'that which protects by being meditated upon'. *(mananAt trAyate iti mantrah).*

This protection by the deity of the *mantra* does not devolve on you until you have sufficiently identified yourself with the *mantra,* heart and soul. Only such a person can be a guru for that *mantra.* The *mantra* itself is considered as the embodiment in sound of some specific deity or supernatural power. So taking the *mantra* by oneself without a guru is disrespect to the *mantra* itself and therefore doubly, a disrespect to the *mantra-devatA* (= the deity of the mantra). Yes, in that sense, the Hindu *mantras* are exclusive, no doubt. But that very fact connotes the sacredness of these mantras. The familiar Gayatri mantra is the most sacred of all these.

CHAPTER 17

Logic of Advaita Part 4

There is another aspect of *mantra* power. The *PuraNas* have several passages where sure redress or healing is promised as the *phala* (fruit) of invoking, chanting or reciting or repeating a specific *mantra* Experts will tell you what *mantra* or what stanza of a certain *stotra* should be invoked for the purpose, what disciplinary observances to follow and what should be offered to the deity formally. Hindu folklore and tradition abound with countless instances of the efficacy of *mantras* and the response of the divine to man's faith and dedication. However, lest we are misunderstood as revelling only in folklore and mythology, here is a dramatic instance of the efficacy of *mantra* even in the modern age, – to which this author was a participant and eye-witness.

The time was around 7-30 in the evening, during the nineteen-fifties, on one of the days of the Navaratri festival when the Mother Goddess is propitiated elaborately in all Hindu homes and temples with great zeal and devotion all over the country. The locale was the outermost corridor called *ADi veedi*, open to the sky, of the Minakshi temple at Madurai in Tamilnadu. Several thousands had gathered to listen to the daily lectures of Sengalipuram Anantarama Dikshidar, specially arranged as a nine-day series *(navAham)* during the festival. But as fate would have it, along with the people sitting on the Adi Veedi, several threatening dark clouds had also gathered in the sky, as if they also wanted to listen to the lectures of the renowned Dikshidar. Thunder boomed; the clouds seemed about to burst. Restlessness spread through the crowd and it seemed that, at any moment, they would decide to disperse, though reluctantly. Were the gods going to disturb the *navaham* and allow the clouds to burst? It certainly looked like it. There was no place in the covered portion of the temple to accommodate the thousands who had gathered in the open corridor.

Dikshidar came a little ahead of time, occupied his seat on the dais, and in his characteristic resounding voice urged the audience to repeat with him the following line from Lalita Sahasranama:

jwAlA-mAlinikA-kshipta-vahni-prAkAra-madhyagA

The chorus rang out and clear. Inspired by Dikshidar, the chanting took on a greater and greater intensity. The same line was repeated perhaps some twenty times. It was a thrilling scene to watch, participate and witness

– the clouds dispersed and the sky became clear. The day's lecture was delivered as usual. The line from Lalita Sahasranama only means:' She (the Goddess) is seated amidst a massive fortress of fire called *jvAlA-MAlini'*. There are also other esoteric meanings of this half-verse, but, as we saw, it was not necessary to know the meaning to get the effect of the *mantra,* for except the Dikshidar and some learned members of the audience, the several thousands of the masses who joined in the chanting could not have known what it meant.

In the personal experience of the author, the same *mantra* was used by this author for a similar purpose with the same effect. It was Shivaratri day, 25th February 1979. It was around 7-30 in the morning. A three-hour special Sai Bhajan was scheduled to start in another half hour in the open corridor of the Saraswati temple in Pilani, Rajasthan, India. The author and a few friends were setting up the place for the Bhajan, hanging pictures of gods, decorating them with flowers, spreading mats and durries, in short making all the preliminary arrangements for the gathering of devotees, expected to number 100 to 150. From the morning, the sky had been clouded, but, as it was not a season for rain, nobody took any notice. But, as the final arrangements were being made, the clouds gathered in great strength and it was surely going to rain. In fact, a few drops were already on the ten or so volunteers who were working. It was suggested that they repeat the half verse starting with *jvAlA-MAlinikA*. The advice was taken by the others and each one, in his own individual way repeated the chanting of the line to himself. It did rain around five minutes to eight, but only for a minute or two. The clouds passed away and the bhajan went on uninterruptedly as scheduled. And, believe it or not, after the bhajan was over, in the afternoon of that day, it did rain and that too really hard.

> **Question 6:** Cannot all this be mere coincidence? Are you not attaching too much importance to your *mantras?* What is the scientific basis for a belief which just connects two unconnected events and calls them cause and effect?

It is good to question the scientific basis on which one attributes a cause and effect relationship to two apparently unconnected events in view of one's faith in religion. In fact the more comprehensive question is: Can science and religion both be true in the same system of Man's knowledge? In other words could that composite system afford to have internal contradictions?. We shall take up that question a little later. Right now we shall touch upon the question of coincidence. How can we ever disprove that the sequence of the two events, namely the chanting of the *mantra* and the holding off of the rain, was only a chance sequence? The fact that one followed the other in both the examples cited may, after all, be only a chance happening. The only scientific way to tackle such problems is to collect a mass of statistical data and apply the theories of statistical inference. But, for the same sequence of two events we may not be able to get enough statistical data – and that is where your attempt to 'prove' or 'disprove' it scientifically will fail. But what one might do is to go to a place where religiously attuned people congregate almost daily – like the Ramanashram, Aurobindo Ashram, or any of the places where the Shankaracharyas camp and the like. Stay in one such place for several weeks and listen to the religious experiences of the varied people that come there. Probe, sift the frills and decorations that usually attach themselves to such stories, keep an open mind and try to find the undercurrent of truth and faith that runs through them all. That is where you will come face to face with 'unbelievable' experiences of mankind, which can never be tested under the conditions of a scientific laboratory, but which also cannot be disproved or discarded as just a mythical experience, because the person who has experienced it is sitting before you, right there, and relating it. The very largeness of such experiences coming from entirely unrelated people will overwhelm you.

If you want to collect a lot of information about cricket experience you have to go and mingle with cricketeers and cricket fans, have'nt you? If you are a journalist wanting to write a knowledgeable article about the underworld, would you not go and be with the underworld for some time before you write the article? So also if you want to collect reliable information about religious experience, there is no other way but to go to such places as mentioned and talk with people who have had the experience. That is what Paul Brunton (1898-1981) did and by his masterly expositions he introduced Ramana Maharishi and the Kanchi Kamakoti Shankaracharya (1894–1994) to the western world. Certainly you will have to contend with the natural human weakness for exaggerating the intensity of an experience and as a scientific modern, you should be able to sift the grain from the chaff.

> **Question 7:** All that you have said simply means that one should abandon scientific rationality and have faith in the mysterious and the miraculous and expect Divinity to come to the rescue. Is this possible in this modern world? And is it desirable? Would it not be foolish to try to move civilization backwards in time?

Your assumption that one should have faith is correct. But your concurrent assumption that one should abandon scientific rationality is wrong. <u>Scientific rationale is not opposed to spiritual pursuit. Scientific rationalism is not an all-embracing methodology. It has its limitations.</u> For instance, no amount of science can explain why a mother is devastated when she hears that the plane in which her son was travelling has crashed, or, for that matter, why she feels supremely happy, if, afterwards she learns that her son was not in that flight. Somewhere along the line in these explanations you would come across concepts like affection, agony, anguish, worry etc. These cannot be formulated with scientific precision.

During the last one hundred and fifty years a remarkable religious renaissance has taken place in India and this is important for all mankind. The important figures involved in this new awakening are all well-known. Every one of these great personalities has emphasized in unmistakable terms the need to stick to certain religious values, deeply embedded in the age- old philosophy of the Upanishads. The total effect of this renaissance is that India has been able to tell the world confidently that science should outgrow its nineteenth century materialistic all-embracing arrogance and assume the humility that physics itself learnt the hard way during the first half of the twentieth century. One's very living is a series of actions. In order to act one must make choices and to make choice one must have a code of values. To arrive at such a code one must know what he is, where he comes from and where he is headed and to what purpose. Without such a code of values rooted in man's faith in his own divine Self, no disease of the world can be cured. No scientific advance can fight the evils prevalent in the society without a parallel advance in Man's evolutionary ascent to the divine.

It is worthwhile at this stage to clear the cobwebs of tremendous disbelief that plague the conscience of many a student of science regarding religion.

Religion is not just rituals and miracles though these figure prominently in all popular religion. Science is one kind of response of the finite to the infinite and religion is another. <u>While science may inform you well, it is religion that can transform you.</u> Certainly a scientist must be on guard against the superficial view, exaggerated emphasis, the imprecise statement, the unsound premise, the unreported fact, fallacious reasoning and the distorted picture. But while guarding against such unscientific practices, the scientist should not fall into the same error as the religious fanatic, who doggedly clings to his dogma. So when a mystic reports his experience which, from the scientific viewpoint and methodology is not verifiable or repeatable, we should, as true scientists, be able to accept that there could be things which we cannot explain. *buddheH paraM buddhvA,* says the Gita (3-43). The New Testament also has a similar thought: *St. Paul (1 Corinthians 2:11-14):* Spiritual verities are not of human wisdom but revealed by God!

Mathematics also has a lesson to teach us in this respect. Suppose I open an algebra book at random and I find a statement there saying

$$5 \times 3 = 1 = 5 + 3$$

I cannot immediately conclude that there is a total absurdity here and so it must be either a printing error or the author must be a crank. For, if I look carefully into the pages preceding the statement somewhere there might be a statement saying, 'In what follows, all our arithmetical calculations are made modulo 7'. This means, in calculating with numbers we discard multiples of 7 and take only the remainder. Thus 5 x 3, which is 15, becomes 1 (after discarding 14) and 5 + 3 which is 8, also becomes 1 (after discarding 7) and both are equal! Incidentally, this kind of algebra is very much at the foundation of the modern theory of coding and transmission of messages across space.

> **Question 8:** In your example about 5 and 3 giving a product as well as a sum equal to 1, you had only given different meanings to 5 and 3. If you give the same meanings to 5 and 3 as everybody gives, you cannot get this kind of contradiction.

I am not giving different meanings. I am giving them the same normal meanings as everybody gives but I am putting them through a process which you did not know or think of earlier. Once you understand my process, my algebra, then you can see that 5 x 3 and 5 + 3 could be the same though ordinarily they are not.

Thus, when a scientist hears a mystic talking about the Inner Self, he has no grounds for asserting that the mystic is talking nonsense. It is a different algebra that the mystic is talking about. He is talking about a different process to be applied to the body, the senses, the mind and the intellect and this results, according to him, in the realization of the Inner Self. The Scientist should not fall into the very superstition against which he warned his fellow beings for centuries. He cannot contend that, since the concept of an inner self appears to contradict his scientific rationale, it is wrong. This was just the attitude taken by 16th century priests towards Copernicus. 'Just because it contradicts our religious beliefs and scriptures, it cannot be right' said the priests. The Subject of the Inner Self of Man is not in the field of Science; it is the field of Vedanta.

Question 9: Does it mean then that in Vedanta there is no scientific proof of its metaphysical statements?

Proof there is – but hold a minute before I tell you where the proof comes from. However, in asking for a scientific proof you are slipping into a trap. You are looking for the answer in the wrong direction. We are not talking about science here. We are talking about the *shAstra* of the Inner Self where the axioms are different.

Where then does the proof come from? This is the grandest feature of Hindu religion and philosophy. It explains why Hinduism does not depend, for establishing its truth, on some event or the life story of some person or persons; why the progress of science can never be inimical to the principles and pursuit of Hinduism which holds that the great truths which are its essence can be realized by one's own intuition. We do not have to dilate on what these truths are. They are the concluding assertions of the Upanishads about the Atman, the permanent substratum, the one invariant entity that survives all the fluctuations and changes that are characteristic of the world within and the world without. The Philosophy of non-duality asserts, with the authority of the Upanishads, that this truth can be realized by oneself through intuition if one practises the discipline which the scriptures have elaborated in every detail. And once this experience of divine communion is there, one can train oneself to remain in that state of eternal existence in union with the Atman even though one is going about the worldly duties and obligations. In this sense Hinduism gives you the privilege of 'seeing' for yourself what the scriptures are talking about. There is no greater proof than seeing for oneself. <u>Thus Vedanta may be called the science of the Inner self.</u> For when all this experimentation goes on in the realms of the Inner Self, the Inner Self unfolds itself, as it were! All this is unbelievable, says the critic and he adds: How can I believe it when I have no such experience? Obviously this criticism is like my village astrologer's naïve opposition to my statement that Saturn has rings! He would not believe me even when I promise to show him the rings through the telescope of the observatory. He thinks he could believe it only if he sees it with his own eyes and not through an instrument, which 'may be doing some trick'! Your disbelief of the mystic's word is exactly like this. What right do you have to tell mystics like Aurobindo that what he says is a figment of his imagination? If you are a good scientist, the most that you can do is to get away by saying, 'Well, I don't understand your Aurobindo's experiment!'.

The spiritual experiences of the Vedantic seers of Hinduism – like *Agastya, Janaka, Kapila, Markandeya, Narada, Parasara, Patanjali, Vyasa, Vasishta, Sanatkumara, Uddalaka and Yajnavalkya* - are all recorded in our scriptures. Each one of them is an authority on spiritual matters. Scientists and teachers of science in modern times who vouchsafe to the dual behaviour of light may not have themselves carried out the two-hole experiment which validates it. They rely on other scientists who have done the experiment and recorded their results. Also there are several other more easily verifiable results which are consequences of the dual behaviour of light and so, even though the whole concept is bizarre, scientists accept it as a fact of science. In the same manner ordinary people do not have to be able to have a direct confirmation of spirituality or of the fact there is a mystic power beyond our rationale. In historical times, over the past twenty centuries, there have been great devotees of the Lord whose devotion to the Lord is as great, if not greater, as the devotion of the greatest Nobel-Laureates of science. They have affirmed many spiritual truths by their intuition. Just a run through the names of these towering giants of spirituality would itself be impressive if not overwhelming. Each one of them is a divine integrator who contributed to the growth of spirituality in this land of India in no small measure. They all breathe the spirit of genuine mystical devotion, sometimes born of a naïve theory of surrender, sometimes born out of the loftiest intellectual conviction, and very often, of both. No amount of historical, archaeological, sculptural or literary research can supersede what they have declared from their spiritual intuition.

CHAPTER 18

A Nine-Point Master Plan for Value Education to Be Symbiotically Embedded in the Educational System

Man's essential qualities are the most welcome qualities of sympathy, compassion, kindliness and brotherhood. These are so because from one point of view his essential core is itself divine and from another point of view man is the child of God created in His own image. It is necessary to tap these qualities of Man in each one of his dealings as a member of the family, of the Nation, of the World.

To do this there is no better way than to delve into the biographies of as many great men of the world as possible - scholars, saints, innovators, leaders, reformers, religious heads, social workers, scientists, devotees of the Lord, writers, poets, thinkers, philosophers, performers of the arts, managers, administrators, entrepreneurs, and professionals. At every level of education of the student, Biography should form part of the compulsory portion of his studies, as one more subject like Mathematics and

Social Sciences. It is not enough to be just part of his study of Language or Literature. As he rises up in the levels, study of biographies under Biography could become more and more detailed. Ultimately when he completes his education, maybe as a professional, doctor, engineer, manager or what-have-you, he should be able to say that he has specialized in (or has put in a certain amount of intensive study in) certain biographies, not necessarily directly related to his profession or calling. For instance, it could be Mahatma Gandhi, J.N. Tata, St. Francis of Assissi, Abraham Lincoln, Mother Theresa, U.V. Swaminatha Iyer, Benjamin Franklin, Cecil Rhodes, Swami Sivananda Madam Curie or Guru Nanak, or scores of others. Lessons from Biography could be the greatest lessons that a child picks up. So the fundamental difference between the present-day curriculum and this proposed curriculum is that in every class from the 4th standard (or grade) to the 12th standard (or grade) there would be one more compulsory subject called 'Great Lives' or 'Biography'. To that extent, the load from the other subjects has to be reduced. It does not matter. We are teaching too much too badly, anyway – and in India at least, we are surviving, because, we are doing that to too few.

Education from the primary level should start with the concept of the whole world/planet as a single entity. At each stage of the development of the story of man there should be less emphasis on nationhood and a greater emphasis on world citizenship, environment and human behavior. Most of the social evils of the adult population may be traced to the fact that the mind refuses to rise from the little world of the individual and one's immediate kith and kin and friendship. The correction for this has to start from childhood and at school.

The habit of book reading should be encouraged on a warfront from childhood upward. It should not matter what book the child reads. Reading, comprehension, the art of communicating with others what has been assimilated by reading, and, in due time, writing – should form part of the compulsory curriculum all the way up even after the student has started narrowing down and specializing. Right now book reading is left, if at all, as an optional and voluntary activity. It would be necessary to institute special awards for this activity and bring it into the mainstream of the student's career in school. It may be said that the modern means of passing information and literature through the facilities provided by Information Technology like the Internet, have compensated the need to go to books and that the Internet has taken over the need for readers to go to books. But the compensation is not adequate enough. Kids use the Internet only to cull out information for their favourite projects either given by their curriculum needs or motivated by their own pet fantasies. They do not stay with the Internet long enough to gulp whole books of substance. Unless kids learn to sit with books and think leisurely on what they have read the thinking habit will get muzzled up. The very Internet that has done all this should now be used to make the student go back to books. Books can be reviewed, summarized, focussed, and recommended by the teachers of the particular locale or school or college. Each educational institution can discover its own means to draw attention to the books that they want their students to read, provide competition for such reading on the Internet itself by announcing awards and incentives. Several innovative measures must be found out as suits the context and the neighborhood. Several commercial booksellers and publishers are doing a wonderful job now on the Internet to draw the attention of those who surf on the net. But non-profit organizations like educational institutions, teachers, professors, thinkers, parent-teacher-associations, social workers and professionals should make it a mission to tell the next generation what to read, how to read and why. If we do not do all this, the twenty-second century citizen in his thirties and forties would not know what to do with a book! And in a century after that, whatever that remains of 'man' will have to start reinventing reading and writing(!) which is probably one of the few things left yet, that distinguishes man from animal.

From the age of 5, the practice of silent prayer should become a daily routine irrespective of the denomination or religion to which the child belongs or does not belong. The value of prayer can never be overstated.

No one can reveal God to another. But by revealing the value of prayer and inculcating the habit of prayer we place the child in a position to receive God-experience, in due time. Spiritual experience can come only through the correct understanding of prayer. Prayer is the point of contact with God. Silent prayer is the preparation of consciousness for the experience of Divinity within. The child should be tuned up from childhood well enough so that at adult age it is ready to receive the inevitable message that unhappiness and suffering are necessary for the unfolding of the soul within and to stand that unhappiness and suffering, prayer is the nutrition needed. So much does not have to be told to the child; but the habit of prayer must be made a second nature. This should not be left for the child to learn by itself after it reaches adult age – as is the experience of many a materialist adult who has learnt things the hard way and then, turned to the ways of the Orient in the past few decades. This is where it is not possible to accept the plea of the rationalist that, to pray or not to pray should be left to the individual for a decision on his own, when he becomes an adult. The plea assumes that each man, without standing on the shoulders of the men of earlier times, begins all over again to learn all that the earlier civilization has already discovered and recorded for us to take the torch from there. That is not the way Man has ascended to the present state of knowledge.

From the age of 7, children should know and learn the habit of sitting for an introspection and meditation.

Any time the child errs in its social habits, obligations, table manners, discipline or routine, it should not receive corporal punishment but only an opportunity to introspect. The habit of introspection has all but disappeared in this modern age when everybody uses more than his leisure time to sit glued to the idiot box, without ever devoting any time to think about anything, not to speak of oneself – except of course, when they worry about something, which any way is not a productive activity.

From the age of 11 onwards, regular lessons on meditation should form part of the curriculum. Meditation need not be sectarian. But meditation is an effort to be done at the individual level and since Indian culture has an under-current of unity in spite of its plurality of traditions, it should be possible certainly in India which has the advantage of several religions coexisting over the centuries, to integrate sectarian meditation into a classroom activity.

From the age of 15, the child should be educated on the positive aspects – not the bizarre, not the fantastic, not the strange, habits and customs – of all world religions by competent teachers, who, while they themselves would be students of comparative religion, would keep their own bias, if any, towards a particular faith or opinion, in abeyance as best as possible in order to present objectively the commonness of spirituality in all religions. Comparative religion is not competitive religion. Every religion is a blend of macro principles and micro setting. The latter is a mixture of local mythology and ritual and this never appeals to a stranger or outsider. Only a powerful poet, a talented sculptor or a mystic sage may be able to impart some understanding of it to one not born and nurtured in the tradition. But the macro-principles are usually understood, at least as an all-embracing framework, though not followed in its totality, because it speaks to man as man. It is a crisis of intellect that wants to adjudicate among the great religions of the world. What is important for the 22nd century citizen is to come together and rediscover that this crisis of intellect can be resolved only by going back to the very ancient thoughts that have remained with us for more than twenty centuries now. The period of the first millenium BC is the most important period of history in this connection. That was the time when the axis of the world's thoughts shifted from a study of nature to the study of man's life and his inner aspirations. Then in India we had the Upanishadic Seers, Mahavira the Jina and Gautama the Buddha; in China we had Lao Tse and Confucius; in Iran there was Zoroaster, in Israel there were the great prophets; and in Greece, Pythagoras, Socrates and Plato. That surge of activity and investigation and the profundity of thought of that period have never since been matched. They achieved so much with so little help from any gadgetry – which, by the way is what is helping us today to unravel further frontiers of knowledge. The philosophers of the first millenium BC achieved what they did by sheer rational thinking coupled with a certain unique intuition of their own. The test of significance of what they left for posterity is in the fact that they have survived twenty centuries of war and peace, strife and hatred, and all the ups and downs of great empires and civilizations. It is extremely doubtful whether anything of what we call 20th and 21st centuries science and technology will survive as valid knowledge twenty centuries hence! The best guess is that not much of what we hold as science today will survive that long and even what we today call the scientific attitude may mean something entirely different in the year 4000 AD

It all means that we, as world-citizens should have a great pride in the universal heritage of religion and spirituality. This has to be passed on to our youngsters not just because it is great history and tradition but because there is a danger of humanity destroying itself by gradual erosion of these ancient roots. Our religions are our best heritage and safest savior. To say, however, that only the macro-principles of these religions are important is to ignore in the context of a tree the sun and soil from which it draws its sustenance. At the same time any emphasis on the micro-setting should not lead one to nurture an aggressive pride in one's culture and nationality. Pride in one's culture and nationality should only be like pride in one's own mother. This pride, to quote Huston Smith (Religions of Man, New American Library, 1958, p.17), should be 'an affirmative pride born of a gratitude for the values he has gained and not a defensive pride whose only device for achieving the sense of superiority it pathetically needs is by grinding down others through invidious comparison'. His roots in his family, his community, his civilization will be deep, but in that very depth he will strike the water table of man's common humanity and thus nourished will reach out in more active curiosity, more open vision, to discover and understand what others have seen'.

In most human cultures religion and culture are highly interwoven; more so in India where religion has been the dominant feeling for centuries. If we build our educational system on the premise that religion is a personal matter students will be left out without the means of understanding any culture beyond a limited subset of their own. Already we see the effect of this error in the educational set-up of the developed countries. The freedom to present a wide spectrum of human belief within a common scholastic context is a major advantage. The fact that in the Indian milieu this wide spectrum is already in the atmosphere should be considered as a great asset rather than a handicap.

History should be studied not as history of the different countries but as history of man and as the history of wars against poverty, disease and wickedness. History should bring out the perspective that peace is not absence of war but peace is a mutual understanding of each other's aspirations and rights. Every period of history should be studied as part of a world history from this point of view and not as part of a nation's struggle for domination or ascent to power. The individual histories of each nation in all its details should not have to be studied until the student reaches adult age.

This is the suggestion of a Master Plan for embedding the spiritual and human values in the educational system. If this can be implemented we would be turning out world-citizens who would also be a citizen of the world of Spirituality. It would not then be difficult to mould such a citizen into a rounded personality whose every work in the world would be a *yAjnA* in the spirit of the Bhagavad-Gita. For such a person, in the words of Sri Aurobindo, (The Synthesis of Yoga by Shri Aurobindo, Aurobindo Ashram, Pondicherry, Third Impression, 1984, pp.132-133), the mental and physical sciences which examine into the laws and forms and processes of things, those which concern the life of men and animals, the social, political and linguistic and historical and those which seek to know and control the labours and activities by which man subdues and utilizes his world and environment, and the noble and the beautiful Arts which are at once work and knowledge, – for every well-made and significant poem, picture, statue or building is an act of creative knowledge, a living discovery of the consciousness, a figure of Truth, a dynamic form of mental and vital self-expression, – all that seeks, all that finds, all that voices or figures is a realization of something of the play of the Infinite and to that extent can be made a means of God-realization or of divine formation.

OM SHANTIh SHANTIh SHANTIh

Index

K

Kalpa, 150
kArana, 78–79
Kenopanishad, 162–164
Kshara purusha, 72
KUtastha, 70–71

M

Madhura bhakti, 131
Mahabharata, 24, 61–62
Mahaswami of Kanchi, 120
MAyA, 71, 78–81, 89, 106, 113, 174–178, 182
Mithya, 75, 107–108, 175, 178

N

Nimbarka, 127
Nirguna brahman, 164, 171, 173

P

ParA bhakti, 95
Paramarthika satta, 166
Political evils, 12, 34
Prahlada, 24
PraNava, 173
prArabdha karma, 74, 83
prAtibhAsika satta, 166, 174

R

Ramana Maharishi, 66, 94, 189
Ramanuja, 98, 101–102, 105, 125, 159
Ramayana, 24, 129

S

Sadashiva brahmendra, 108
Saguna brahman, 77, 171–173, 177–178
Samarth Ramdas, 132
Samsara, 36, 66, 89, 94, 98, 135, 140
Samyama, 90
Sathya Sai Baba, 58
Shakti PraNava, 173
Sthula, 78
Sukshma, 78
Svabhava, 90
Swami Chinmayananda, 150
Swami Vivekananda, 119, 178

T

Tukaram, 132
Turiya Avastha, 171
Turiya Avastha, 171

U
UpAya, 126
Upeyam, 126

V
Valmiki, 25
VAsanas, 12, 20, 39, 53,
    71, 74–75, 79, 82, 87,
    90, 94, 139–140, 145,
    155, 173

Vedanta Desika, 127
Visishtadvaita, 98, 103,
    105
Vivarana school, 69–70
Vyasa, 25, 195

Y
Yajna, 138–141, 143–148,
    150–151, 156, 206